Zeitschrift für Kunst- und Kulturwissenschaften

Mitteilungsorgan des Ulmer Vereins –
Verband für Kunst- und Kulturwissenschaften e.V.

kritische berichte

Heft 3   2012   Jahrgang 40

Bildende Künste und	Robert Felfe	Editorial	3
Dynamiken der Natur	Claudia Swan	Memory's Garden and other Wondrous Excerpts: Ernst Brinck (1582–1649), Collector	5
	Robert Felfe	Naturabgüsse – künstliche Zeugung und Kreisläufe des Lebens	21
	Nikola Irmer	Promethean Boldness	36
	Henrike Haug	«Wunderbarliche Gewechse». Bergbau und Goldschmiedekunst im 16. Jahrhundert	49
	Joris van Gastel	Geology and Imagery in the Kingdom of Naples: A Letter on the Origins of Alabaster (1696)	65

Robert Felfe
Bildende Künste und Dynamiken der Natur
Editorial

Das vorliegende Heft beleuchtet einen markanten Schnittpunkt mehrerer Forschungsperspektiven, die in jüngerer Zeit große Aufmerksamkeit fanden. Zum einen ist dies die Geschichte des Sammelns in der Frühen Neuzeit. Seit den 1980er Jahren sind Sammlungen der Renaissance und des Barock verstärkt Gegenstand intensiver Studien. Die *Kunstkammer* ist dabei nicht nur in den Fokus historischen Interesses gerückt, sondern wird vielfach als Typus und Modell musealer Präsentation diskutiert und aufs Neue erprobt. Bezeichnend für die frühneuzeitliche Sammlungspraxis waren wiederum die Interaktionen und Verschränkungen zwischen künstlerischer Praxis, dem Wissen über Natur sowie kunsttheoretisch-ästhetischem Denken.

Eine der zentralen Fragen, um die es in den beiden skizzierten Themenfeldern geht, richtet sich auf die spezifische Rolle, die die Künste – ihre Verfahren wie auch ihr theoretisches Selbstverständnis – in diesem Zusammenhang spielen. Das nahezu unerschöpfliche Material für konkrete Fallstudien bringt häufig ebenso einzigartige wie überraschende Einblicke. Die Suche nach systematischen Momenten des Zusammenhangs bewegt sich daher über weite Strecken noch immer auf offenem Terrain. Wenn es stimmt, dass die Künste und das Sammeln am Wissen über Natur *nicht* nur auf die Weise partizipieren, dass sie diese irgendwie wiedergeben, darstellen, vermitteln etc., sondern selbst mit hervorbringen, dann ist möglichst präzise zu zeigen, wie dies geschieht. Es ist hinlänglich bekannt, *dass* Künste und Wissenschaften im 16. Und 17. Jahrhundert keine kategorial unterschiedenen Tätigkeitsfelder waren – wie aber lässt sich dieses Nicht-Getrennt-Sein beschreiben und welche Bewegungen fanden hier statt?

Vor diesem Hintergrund konzentrieren sich die Beiträge dieses Heftes entweder auf einzelne, bislang unbekannte Quellen oder aber auf in dieser Hinsicht besonders signifikante Kunstwerke. Im Wirkungskreis so bekannter Topoi wie dem der Analogie von *natura* und *ars*, von Mikro- und Makrokosmos lenken sie den Blick auf historische Gefüge von künstlerischer Arbeit als Wissen über die Natur, auf Methoden der Wissensorganisation und Facetten ästhetischer Reflexion. Verschiedene soziale Milieus folgten dabei verschiedenen Vorlieben und Ambitionen, bildeten verschiedene ‹kognitive Stile› aus. Und doch zeichnet sich eine Signatur ab, die die auf den ersten Blick disparaten Gegenstände und Phänomene verbindet. Zwischen universellen Wissenskonzepten, deren Ansprüche sich zunehmend schwerer einlösen ließen, und den offensichtlichen Grenzen menschlicher Vermögen wie der Erinnerung, setzten künstlerische Arbeit und eine weitgefächerte empirische Sensibilität als spezifisches Potential der Imagination eine eigene Dynamik in Gang, die das Wissen über Natur im Detail wie auch strukturell veränderte.

46   Van eenige dingen, die men tot een memorie
      heeft willen bewaren

Te Mompellier in Franckrijck wert alsnoch bewaert
In de Medicine die gene die aldaer gedoctoreert werden, den Pluen
den wode rock van François Rabelais, moetende alle
aentrocken.

Te Prag in der Hussiten kercke plachten te hang-
en die Cerimonialia van Joannes Huss, gelijck ich
pater Pluen oock aldaer gesien hebbe, aº 1615.

Te Cöuln in der Apostels kerck, heb ich oock
aº 1614 noch sien hangen het webbe doecks,
twelck een vrouw aldaer, nadien sij van haere
begraefnisse weder opgestaen was, gesponnen
hadde.

Te Padua in der Augustijner kercke, werde ons aº 1614 oock noch getoont den
predigstoel, daerop D. Martinus Lutherus hadde
plach gepredickt, als hij daerdoor naer Roma
reijsde.

Te Leyden wert oock alsnoch bewaert bij
de Steermakers Gilde de tafel, op de welcke
eertijts Johan van Leyden gewercht ende sijn
ambacht gedaen hadde.

Claudia Swan
Memory's Garden and other Wondrous Excerpts:
Ernst Brinck (1582–1649), Collector

That exotic, preternatural, curious, and/or wondrous items were regarded in the early modern era with interest unto compulsion is by now a familiar feature of the historical landscape. In the sixteenth and seventeenth centuries throughout Europe princes, pharmacists, patricians, painters, and others assembled collections of varying degrees of grandeur and varying scales; they have come to be known as ‹Kunstkammern›, ‹Wunderkammern›, or ‹cabinets of curiosity›. These vast compilations contained varied entities ranging from natural items (*naturalia*) and man-made objects (*artificialia*) to non-European goods (*exotica/ethnographica*) and instruments (*scientifica*). Over the past decades a great deal of scholarly attention has been paid to these collections, highlighting such facets of the phenomenon as the relationship between collecting and knowledge; the relationship between collecting and power; the sociology of collecting; the religious, political, professional dimensions of collections—to name a few. Occasionally, discussions revert to a theme introduced a century ago in the landmark study by Julius von Schlosser—namely, the national or regional character of collecting practices.[1]

This essay profits from the generous literature to date and the range of subjects it encompasses, in order to introduce the all but unknown early modern Dutchman and collector Ernst Brinck (1582–1649).[2] What follows is a prolegomenon to an ongoing study of Brinck, whose literary legacy comprises an extraordinary resource for the study of seventeenth-century practices as varied and as interconnected as reading, collecting, diplomacy, trade, and travel—and more. While early modern collecting was an international phenomenon whose success depended on the cultivation of networks reaching across local, national, and even global terrains and borders, Dutch collecting practices tend to be studied locally and relatively speaking less avidly than other European instances of early modern curiosity in practice.[3] Among other things, this introduction to one aspect of Brinck's many pursuits aims to help redress this imbalance.

The Dutch landscape of collecting

Dutch collections of naturalia and remarkable specimens assembled by the textile merchant Levinus Vincent (1658–1727) and the medical doctor Frederick Ruysch (1638–1731) or the mayor of Amsterdam, traveler, and maecenas Nicolaes Witsen (1641–1717) are relatively familiar landmarks of the European phenomenon writ large.[4] These later seventeenth-century collections were widely renowned in their own time. In scope and character they bridge the gap between the Renaissance ‹studioli› and post-Enlightenment museums of natural history. Early seventeenth-century Dutch collections such as Ernst Brinck's have left a considerably lighter mark in the historical record. They were not open to a paying public, as was Vincent's, for example, and although Brinck's contemporary and friend Bernardus Paludanus (1550–1633), city doctor in Enkhuizen and fabled collector, did attract visitors from far and wide, the learned Dutch gentleman's collection was not, in the early seventeenth century, on a par with princely or imperial ambitions. – Cosimo de' Medici visited Dutch collections in 1667–1669, and Ruysch sold his anatomical cabinet to Peter the Great in 1717.[5] – The earlier collections adhered, generally speaking, to the model proposed by Francis Bacon in his *Gesta Grayorum*, where a philosophically inclined counselor proposes that a ruler who would rule by knowledge (of nature, rather than by force, for example) assemble a library, a garden, a collection, and a still house or laboratory. This counselor prescribes

> a goodly, huge Cabinet, wherein whatsoever the hand of man by exquisite art or engine has made rare in stuff, form or motion; whatsoever singularity, chance, and the shuffle of things hath produced; whatsoever Nature hath wrought in things that want life and may be kept; shall be sorted and included.[6]

The landmark 1992 study and exhibition catalogue *De wereld binnen handbereik* picks up speed after mid-century; where earlier collections are cited, they function as harbingers of things to come rather than as the focus of study or analysis. Nonetheless there is evidence that Baconian cabinets were more frequent in early seventeenth-century Holland than generally acknowledged. Eric Jorink's recent study, *The Book of Nature*, describes several such collections, among them Brinck's, for the first time.[7] Even the statesman and man of letters Constantijn Huygens (1596–1687) participated in the phenomenon: in 1630 he wrote that «he himself collected such things, which are contained in over 900 boxes».[8] Huygens's collection has not, however, made more than a cameo appearance in histories of Dutch collecting.

One Dutch collection that does feature in histories of the time, often forming the *terminus post quem* for studies of Dutch collecting, is that of Paludanus.[9] Paludanus traveled widely before taking up that post of city doctor of Enkhuizen in the north of Holland in the 1580s. During his travels in Italy, German territories, eastern Europe, the Middle East, and Egypt, he accumulated not just medical education—he received his doctorate in medicine in Padova—but experience of collections and items for his own collection, the contents of which were predominately natural, generally unusual, and in some cases religious.[10] A contemporary description that survives of a visit in 1594 to this cabinet of wonders gives a vivid sense of the encounter with such a vast assemblage of goods:

> The other day I visited Paludanus […]. He showed me his collection, which had such varied and numerous items that I scarcely believed they existed in nature. Nature herself seems to have moved into his house, entire and unmutilated, and there is nothing written down in books that he cannot present to your eyes. That is why the great man Joseph Scaliger gave all his rarities (which were both numerous and spectacular) to Paludanus, saying, ‹Here are your things, which I have possessed unjustly›.[11]

The Dutch jurist Hugo Grotius (1583–1645) was particularly inspired—or perhaps confused—by Paludanus's extensive possessions, which he described as «Thesaurus Orbis, Totius compendium/ Arca universi, sacra Naturae penus, Templumque Mundi...».[12] Around the turn of the seventeenth century, at a time when he maintained intense contacts and interaction with the merchant-voyager and author Jan Huygen van Linschoten (1562–1611), the ‹Dutch Magellan›, Paludanus began to collect ethnographic items in large numbers for display and study as well. His collection evolved over time, and Paludanus sold it off on at least two occasions prior to his death. His involvement with trade—primarily by way of van Linschoten, and also as a result of his living in a port town, Enkhuizen—and with trade in the East and the North in particular accounts for the inclusion of ethnographica in his collection over time.

Elsewhere, I have written about the Leiden pharmacist Christiaen Porret (1554–1627), and explored some of the ways in which Porret's collection may have functioned.[13] Like Brinck, Porret was known in the seventeenth century but has been overlooked since, and Porret's collection bears recalling by way of introducing Brinck's. On 28 March 1628, within a year of his death, the well-respected pharmacist's collection was put up for auction in Leiden. What became of the stunning range of objects listed under 719 headings in the printed catalogue is not known. The title page of the auction catalogue announces the sale of:

> Exceptional items or curiosities and rare naturalia (*sinnelickheden*) [...]. Indian and other foreign conches/ shells/ terrestrial and sea creatures/ minerals/ and also strange animals; as well as some artfully made handicrafts and paintings/ which Christiaen Porrett [sic], Pharmacist of late/ assembled in his *Cunstcamer*.[14]

Like the phrases on the title page, the entries in the catalogue vacillate between categories in ways that could seem bewildering. However, within the European context of collections assembled in the sixteenth and seventeenth from the courts from Prague and Petersburg to Lisbon and The Hague and in ducal residences in between, as on a smaller scale privately, the combination in Porret's «Cunstcamer» of natural items, works of art and handicraft, ethnographic specimens, and even optical devices is entirely congruent with more general developments. The fact that it was assembled and maintained by a Dutch pharmacist may have doubly condemned it to historical oblivion. Pharmaceutical collections have often been overlooked as ‹mere› professional efforts, rather than as the loci of natural history and natural philosophy, and as hubs of social and trade networks that spread far and wide; and the history of Dutch collecting has, as suggested above, focused on later developments and remained relatively insular.

Ernst Brinck – scholar, traveller and political agent

While Ernst Brinck remains all but unknown to contemporary historians, there is ample evidence that he was well-known among contemporaries and that his collection was renowned. Rather uncannily, the fellow resident of Harderwijk Wolter van Speulde described him in ca. 1700 as

> Mr. Ernst Brinck, mayor of this city during his lifetime and a great researcher of antiquities, who shall be remembered for his unusual knowledge of various languages, his own *Konstcamer* and other curiosities, known through his writings on Harderwijck [sic].[15]

This quotation dates to well after Brinck's death in 1649 and to well before the modern literature made an effort to catch up with his accomplishments in the nineteenth century, and it manages perfectly to capture the salient aspects of his life and remains most pertinent to this article. Brinck was born in Durlach, Germany, to a well-to-do family from Harderwijk. He studied in Leiden and subsequently with the great philologist Isaac Casaubon (1559–1614) in Paris, traveled to Constantinople in the service of the first ambassador of the States General of the Netherlands to the Ottoman Empire, and later served as mayor of Harderwijk, the city from which his family hailed.[16] Brinck's literary remains include annotations, inscriptions, lists, and commentaries contained in his *Adversaria* (nearly fifty notebooks, never previously published or studied in detail) preserved in the regional archives in Harderwijk and three *alba amicorum*, in the collection of the Koninklijke Bibliotheek in The Hague. In the latter three well-preserved volumes Brinck collected signatures over the course of his adult life, beginning in the first decade of the seventeenth century, from anyone who was anyone as well as examples of as many (he claimed) as two hundred languages.[17] Inscriptions and pasted-in portrait prints of Leiden academic luminaries historian Joseph Scaliger (1540–1609), Professor of Greek and Latin Bonaventura Vulcanius (1538–1614), and botanist Carolus Clusius (1526–1609) vie for space in the albums with vividly painted coats of arms of Gelderland nobility Brinck came to know; the signatures of the calligrapher/artist Jan van de Velde (1593–1641), the poet and artist Anna Maria van Schurman (1607–1678), and the composer Jan Pietersz. Sweelinck (1562–1621); and records of encounters with medical professionals and collectors Bernardus Paludanus and Ferrante Imperato (1525?–1615?) in Naples. In his capacity as secretary to the Dutch ambassador in Constantinople, Cornelis Haga (1578–1654), Brinck collected inscriptions during his travels, from samples of foreign script to records of encounters with foreign potentates and in some cases, as in the Ottoman inscription highlighted with gold by the Grand Vizier Halil Pasha (d. 1629), a combination of both. It was during his return to the Netherlands from Turkey via Italy in 1614 that Brinck visited with Imperato in Naples and, in Florence, he met Galileo Galilei, whose signature accompanies an autograph sketch of the moons of Jupiter.[18] Brinck cultivated a vast network of acquaintances with the same zeal with which he collected information—about, for example, the 200 languages he claimed to know of, from Brazilian Pitiguar and the language of peasants in Schlesien to quack-doctor-speak and the «language of Utopia». He also amassed a vast array of curiosities and antiquities, a substantial library, and an expansive garden. Brinck garnered a reputation as a signal figure in Harderwijk, the port town where his family was from and where he served as librarian to the Gymnasium as well as mayor after pursuing his studies and a career as a political agent. Brinck's endeavors—as agent, as collector, as social networker, as librarian, as civic representative, as author—qualify him as a key figure in the networks of knowledge his interests and his experience spanned in early seventeenth- century Europe.

Brinck's notebooks and early modern cultures of collecting
In addition to the *alba amicorum* in The Hague, just under fifty notebooks compiled by Brinck survive.[19] These notebooks, the *Adversaria*, contain extensive textual annotations and observations—sixteen of the notebooks are devoted to annotations on texts, and two additional notebooks contain notes on the Bible; almost just as many pocket-size volumes contain descriptions of local or foreign places Brinck visited. Three volumes contain notes and observations on natural historical subjects—birds, four-footed animals, and fish—and there are many filled with memorabilia, including multiple lists and indices.

The individual notebooks are octavo or duodecimo in format, and run to roughly one hundred folios each; they are bound in parchment; and each of them bears a title penned by Brinck. The titles include, for example, «Observations and Annotations from Various Authors», «Wondrous Observations on the Nature of Some Birds», «Wondrous and memorable accounts of our times». The contents of the individual notebooks bear subtitles or subject headings—for example, «Good times when things were cheap», «Of esteemed pictures», «Of jokes of nature», «Of notable thefts», «Of false witnesses and false trade», «On the human soul», «On thunder and lightning», «Observations on fruits», «Remarkable aspects of flowers», «On princes who practice mechanical arts and various hobbies». Brinck also compiled lists. One notebook contains a plethora of lists. It opens with a list of fish, subdivided in to fish caught in the Zuyderzee and fish brought to market from the sea and proceeds through lists of local animals and birds to names of ships—with individual subheadings for the sorts of ships: those formerly used, vessels currently in use, ships for traveling inland and fishing, river vessels, and smaller ships usually without sails.

There are lists of the names of fruit-bearing trees in the Veluwe, the local landscape, as well as of non-fruit-bearing trees; of berries; of grains and legumes; of names of apples and pears and vegetables and salad herbs that grew in Gelderland; and of the contents of Brinck's garden in 1608 and subsequent years, as well as of the contents of ships returning from the East and West Indies. Brinck's *Adversaria* offer a crucial, vast resource for the reconstruction of the who, what, and when of early modern collecting and trade in exotica: he provides first-hand information about who owned what wondrous objects where; recounts the contents of his virtually unknown collection; records the sale of numerous exotic and luxury goods, such as shells purchased by Marie de' Medici and items sold to Emperor Rudolf II; describes rulers' artisanal skills; notes wondrous objects made of gold, silver, and copper, as well as wondrous smells and sounds. Brinck's notebooks are filled with accounts of trade and global exploits; of wondrous and otherwise noteworthy events; of recently painted works of art in painters' ateliers and of prices fetched at auctions as well. He was an amateur linguist; and he compiled observations on fauna both indigenous and exotic. Throughout the *Adversaria*, Brinck records and participates in the circulation of knowledge in ways that are relevant to the cultural history of early modern science. These notebooks comprise an invaluable ‹ego document› and indefatigable resource for information garnered on the streets of Amsterdam, in the ports of the Republic, in the quiet of Brinck's Harderwijk library, in courts and residences throughout Europe, and in the studious presence of east Indian dried birds' beaks.

While the scope and range of their contents is dizzying—the contents of the *Adversaria* and the three surviving *alba amicorum* comprise a virtual, text-based sort of *Wunderkammer*—Brinck's literary remains were composed and collected in accordance with standard practices of the era. The note-taking and list-making drive in evidence throughout the notebooks is entirely congruent with «repetition and copying out [...] the keystones of Renaissance pedagogy», and the management of information so genially described by Ann Blair.[20] His famous contemporary the virtuoso, scholar, and collector the Frenchman Nicolas Fabri de Peiresc (1580–1637) also assiduously, compulsively took notes—in order to

preserve information from oblivion. Peiresc took notes on sheets of paper, employed scribes to assist, and
> acted as a clearinghouse for all kinds of information, antiquarian and natural philosophical, and regularly entered and retrieved information in his papers to share with others who requested it.[21]

No correspondence from or to Brinck survives; his annotations remained private. It is worth noting that his practice of taking notes resonates with the advice of his Paris mentor Casaubon, also an avid note-taker and author of a commonplace book, who admonished, «Remember to set down everything you read in books of excerpts. This is the only way to aid your failing memory».[22] Early modern humanist pedagogical treatises therefore emphasized the necessity of taking notes for all readers, regardless of whether they were historians or not. «It is no waste of time to take notes», advised one, «but rather to read without taking notes».[23]

The commonplace books or *Adversaria* Brinck composed extend well beyond excerpts from texts, to include all sorts of observations, hearsay, experiences, data: Brinck was an *admirator* and administrator of nature and natural knowledge and his textual remains comprise an archive of early modern knowledge formation, production, and collection.

In ways this article can only adumbrate, Brinck's literary remains are everywhere redolent of the collecting impulse, the drive to compile. He cites contemporary local and foreign events—in one notebook, for example, he lists notable thefts committed in the Netherlands; remarkable events beginning with the baptism of forty children in the Nieuwe Kerk in Amsterdam in 1619; ‹Lusibus naturae› observed in Enkhuizen, in Padova, in Constantinople and elsewhere and in another he lists such «Items worthy of being remembered» as a red cape belonging to Rabelais; a femur bone of Jan Hus in the Hussite Church in Prague, which Brinck visited in 1615; the pulpit from which Martin Luther preached in Padova en route to Rome.[24] The same reportorial mode adheres in Brinck's observations on objects in his and other collections. With a similar commitment to the texture of facts he list objects he observed in the Leiden University anatomical theater, foreign collections, homes of Amsterdam collectors, and among the curiosities belonging to Paludanus in Enkhuizen; Brinck also enumerates and comments on objects in his own vast collection as well as in his garden. With the exception of the garden, the contents of which he recalls in one lengthy passage of a single notebook, the references to objects in his own and other collections are scattered throughout the *Adversaria*, where they are entered under a variety of headings in a number of different locations.

Brinck's literary remains refer to and at the same time embody collecting practices of the early modern era—especially if we understand the accumulation of information by way of note-taking as culturally akin to the practice of collecting. Blair writes that:
> The stockpiling of notes was part of a larger cultural phenomenon of collecting and accumulating in early modern Europe that generated not only textual compilations in manuscript and in print but also collection of natural and artificial objects, from plants and minerals and medals, paintings, and ‹curiosities›.[25]

The preserved literary remains in Harderwijk include clippings from contemporary newssheets as well as individual sheets of notes and lists presumably intended to be processed, entered in to the notebooks in time. One set of unbound

1 Ernst Brinck, *Adversaria*, Harderwijk Gemeentearchief OAH 2024a.

notes on small slips of paper, smaller than the pages in the notebooks, records observations made in Leiden. One sheet contains a list of all of the animals whose skeletons kept in the anatomical theater at the Leiden University, from a whale, ‹in cella›, and a fox to a weasel and a swan, and hastily noted additional objects such as anatomical figures («plurimae Tabulae Anatomicae»), the skin of a human, the bones and teeth of a whale, and anatomical instruments. An additional note records the number of cloth shearers living in Leiden in 1645 (900);

that there were 40 booksellers in Leiden above and beyond the printers; and other local data. A third sheet is covered recto and verso with chorographical notations relating to the holdings of civic institutions (Fig. 1): Brinck notes that the great philologist and antiquarian Joseph Justus Scaliger (1540–1609) left 208 manuscripts to the university library, in a variety of languages; he records having seen various stones and wood in the garden; and he lists a number of wondrous objects in the anatomical theater, a renowned a site of curiosities—Brinck's list includes a mummy, a Roman funeral urn, seven stones removed from the body of Johannes Heurnius (1543–1601), Professor of Medicine at Leiden, shoes from the King of Siam, the wing of a flying fish, a crab from the East Indies, an elephant head brought from Angola in 1620, the head of a tiger, the blood and eye of a crocodile, and such objects, which correspond to early records of the collection housed in the anatomical theater.[26] Brinck studied at Leiden in the first decade of the century, collected numerous signatures from luminaries at the university in 1606, but the notes described here probably date to a later visit. One of the sheets bears Brinck's writing in two different inks—the majority of the notes are in Latin and the later darker emendations are in Dutch—suggesting that he subsequently emended the notes.

It seems likely that these sheets are surviving preliminary notes, made on site in this case, and that Brinck's intention was to enter them in to notebooks later, re-ordering them as he did so. This practice exemplifies contemporary note-taking modes codified in manuals that stressed the importance of recording one's reading experience—and at the same time it goes far beyond humanist reading practice. Brinck's notebooks were structured to serve as digests of larger terrains of knowledge: a library could be condensed, indexed, and referenced by way of excerpts organized in notebooks.[27] Merchants' notebooks were formally analogous, insofar as merchants kept both daily records as well as ledgers in which the journal transactions were indexed according to categories. Data, observations, annotations, sums, experience: all were note-worthy subjects, to be collated and indexed, recalled. Francis Bacon directly compared one of his own notebooks, the «Loose Commentary» of 1608, which contains all manner of data and observations, to a «merchant's waste book, where to enter all manner of *remembrancia* of matter, service, business, study…either sparsim or in schedules, without any manner of restraint».[28]

Language, antiquity, nature and the limits of memory
Eric Jorink, the only scholar who has to date endeavored to describe Brinck's collection, suggests that it was a product of Brinck's philological interests. Brinck was an early modern antiquarian or student of antiquity—hence his interest in languages in general and his qualifications to serve as secretary to the ambassador to Constantinople in particular (Jorink surmises that Brinck knew Arabic and Turkish). It is unclear what Brinck studied formally in Leiden, but he did spend nine months under the tutelage of Casaubon in Paris, and his notebooks are written in a fluid mixture of Latin, Dutch, French, and Italian (diplomatic lingua franca) and contain smatterings of German as well. In addition, he proudly listed in one of the albums presently in the Koninklijke Bibliotheek in The Hague (135 K 4) upwards of 200 languages with which he was familiar. The list, titled «Catalogus Linguaru[m] & varioru[m] dialectoru[m], quoru[m] singularu[m] specimen

extat in meo alba», may have been inscribed on the opening sheets of the volume (fols. 1–3) with the intention of transcribing said specimens in to the album. The list is by and large fluidly composed, the bulk of it having been penned in one go. Later pages of this album contain some specimens of some of the languages listed. The initial folios contain inscriptions in a variety of languages and scripts Brinck collected while he was in Constantinople as secretary to the Dutch ambassador—calligraphy signed by the poet to the Sultan; an entry by Andrea Negroni, ambassador to the Porte, signed in Italian beneath an Arabic inscription dotted in gold ink; inscriptions by the Greek and the Armenian Patriarchs of Constantinople—as well as inscriptions he acquired on his journey home, from Galileo, Imperato, Fabio Colonna, Giovanni Battista della Porta, and others. Other pages contain pasted-in samples of Chinese and Malaysian texts, as well as transcribed specimens of many different scripts, from Utopian (!) and Chaldean to Babylonian and Cabbalistic, and several pages with descriptions of gestures and their meanings in Ottoman/Seraglio Sign language.[29] Brinck's linguistic ambitions echo and are one with his collecting impulse, and the two are forms of a paradigmatic early modern drive to know.

Brinck's collection is no longer; like so many others of its time it survives only on paper. As outlined in the foregoing pages, the form in which it comes down to us, as an assemblage of notes in Brinck's *Adversaria*, is part and parcel of the culture in which the collection was amassed. The remainder of this article will summarize the textual remains of Brinck's collection, touching on the rhetoric of its representation and presenting the general contours of what is preserved, by way of recommending it for future study. Brinck's personal collection is said to have been housed in his library in Harderwijk, where he lived before he departed for Turkey in 1612 and after his return a little over two years later.[30] The majority of Brinck's references to his own collection are undated, but the dates of his observations on other collections suggest that his was a product of the last three decennia of his life. It is clear from his notes that he visited Paludanus's collection in 1610,[31] and his travel notes dating to 1612–1614 are filled with references to collections and curiosities he saw along the way. Those references, a few of which I cite here, are symptomatic of Brinck's interests and at the same time of the contemporary vocabulary relating to the contents and the sites of collections.[32]

In 1614, when Brinck returned from his service in Turkey, he traveled by way of Greece and Italy. In Naples he met the apothecary Ferrante Imperato (1550–1631), and viewed his collection; Imperato signed Brinck's album and although his inscription is undated, Brinck dates their encounter in the volume of his *Adversaria* dedicated to birds: «Anno 1614 heb ik te Napels gesien, auem Trochijlum qua purgat dentes Crocodilorum; in wijtvermaerde constkamer van Fernando Imperato».[33] In the same year, in Rome, he saw, «in the *Cabinett* of Pope Paul V an ostrich egg in which the Passion of Christ was very artfully carved, and another on which the Agnus Dei was engraved, very fine».[34] In his notes on animals, Brinck refers to the «Garderobbe» of the same pope, where he saw a beautiful Rhinoceros horn. In the «Schatkamer» (treasury) of the Grand Duke in Florence, he saw the horns of a male and female rhinoceros; and he mentions visiting Paolo Veneto's «musaeum».[35] His travels also took him to the renowned «Lusthuijss» of the Grand Duke in Pratolino outside Florence, where he viewed many wondrous antiquities and naturalia; Brinck reserved special praise for the aviary, one of many such collections he mentions in a section on «Renowned birdcages».[36] Brinck describes the aviary at Fontainebleau at some length, and his notes include references to an aviary maintained by Prince Maurice in The Hague, as well as to living and stuffed birds and eggs and beaks and nests he observed in Prague and in Rijswijk, in Dresden (a dried phoenix no less!) and in Enkhuizen.[37]

Brinck's *Adversaria* contain references to a range of types of collections—cabinets, treasuries, pleasure gardens, aviaries, menageries, *Kunstkammern*, to the East and West India Company headquarters in Amsterdam (*Oost-Indisch Huis* and *West-Indisch Huis*) as repositories of exotica, from Chinese paintings to shells and more, and even to the «Rustcamer/Wapencamer» (armory) in Dresden, which housed extraordinary feathers of inestimable value.[38] Collectors are referred to by name and/or title and in some cases he refers to anonymous ‹liefhebbers› or ‹amateurs›. Often, when referring to a collector or collection he uses the preposition ‹at› in the sense of ‹chez›—for example: «At D. Paludano in Enkhuizen I saw various beautiful birds of paradise, as also at Mr. Wickefoort in Amsterdam».[39] In references to his own collection, Brinck uses the terms ‹Konstcamer/Constkamer› and ‹Cabinett› regularly and interchangeably.

Brinck's *Adversaria* attest to his having maintained a «goodly, huge Cabinet» with its due share of and sheen. The objects he declares he owned compare well with those collected by his contemporaries Paludanus and Porret: most are natural, some are ancient, and many are exceptional. A poem by the classicist poet Nicolaus Heinsius (1620–1681) refers to Brinck's *Pinacotheca* or *Thesaurum* as containing shells, stones, coins, animals, and all sorts of other things from the entire world; the collection brings together objects from near and far and, as such, offers «an effigy of the world».[40] Brinck's notebook on birds opens with a notation concerning a bird's nest in his ‹Konstcamer›, in a certain box; the nest came from the East Indies where, Brinck writes, it is eaten as well as being used in commerce. The entire thing seems to be covered in wax or resin or lacquer, he notes. In the margin next to this description, Brinck states that the East India Company trades in birds and birds' nests; below this he refers to Ulisse Aldrovandi's *Ornithologiae* (1581), Pedro Teixeira's *Relaciones* (1610), and other texts, lists skeletons of birds in the Leiden University anatomical theater, and describes other nests he owns and has seen.[41] (Fig. 2)

He owned a foot or ankle of an ostrich, as well as seven beautiful ostrich eggs, one of which has a silver cover—it is a drinking vessel of a sort widely familiar in such collections.[42] Brinck owned «one very beautiful» bird of paradise, whose body and feathers he lovingly describes, concluding that it was decorated with at least eight different colors;[43] two very beautiful eagle's claws, the head of an eagle, and a few wings, as well as some bunches of eagle feathers;[44] penguin wings; a parrot egg laid in Kampen; a stone from a bird from Mauritius, a Dodo with medicinal properties; two West-Indian birds and a very small West-Indian bird's head and beak, very beautiful in color, lapis blue and purple;[45] various items made of woven peacock feathers, such as a fan and table coverings and a bunch of white peacock feathers; fourteen small grey, white, and brown stones from the stomach of a korhaan (bustard), «very good eye stones».[46] The collection also contained Egyptian figurines, three armadillos, the teeth of a hippopotamus, a bracelet made of shells, and countless other items, much too numerous to cite

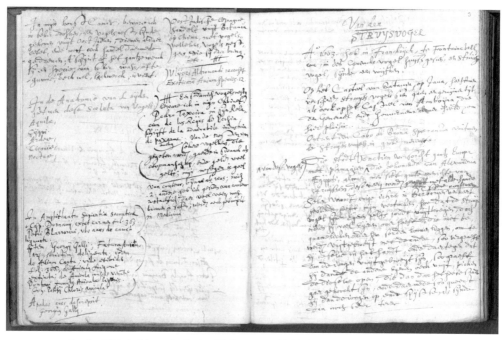

2 Ernst Brinck, *Adversaria*, Harderwijk Gemeentearchief OAH 2057 2v and 3 r.

here. The contents of Brinck's collection are natural and preternatural, but not unusual for the time. They are only incidentally artistic or artificial: an ostrich egg set in silver, for example, or woven peacock feathers. Brinck writes about works of art in his *Adversaria*, but his collecting impulse did not extend to the domain of the visual arts.

A great deal more remains to be said about Brinck's collection. One notable aspect of his notes is the form of attention so vivid in the descriptions of objects in his possession; the descriptions are often most precise in the specification of color and frequently refer to the beauty of the objects. This is an *aesthetic morphology* that finds its counterpart in the work of Carolus Clusius for example—a figure Brinck rather surprisingly does not cite much if at all. These are not the only features of the rhetoric and structure of the descriptions in his *Adversaria* that are striking, however. Two aspects of the remains of Brinck's collection seem especially worthy of attention here. First, his records of objects in his own collection are interwoven with references to other objects in other collections, in a way that embodies and in a sense re-activates the patterns of observation and description and association that structured early modern natural inquiry. Consider, for example, the presentation of information about the bird of paradise, cited and illustrated above. Brinck's descriptions of the peacock feather objects in his collection are likewise set in a ‹pastiche› of commentary that ranges, in this case, from courtly use of peacock feather fans at German courts and woven items made from the quills of the feathers to practices for obtaining white peacocks. Brinck writes that, according to German practice, to obtain a white peacock one should lay down white sheets when the bird broods eggs or paint the walls white, as this will have the necessary effect on the imagination to change the color of the eggs. Brinck notes on this same page that he saw in 1614 in the collection of Pope Paul V «an altar, very beautifully woven of only peacock feathers, ad so artfully done that the image appears to have been painted». Immediately following this note, Brinck describes peacock flesh as rather yellow and difficult to digest.[47] The object at hand, the bird in this case, the peacock, is a sort of mirror, directing refracting observations that call up and cull from past experience, practices, and text. This is but one example, peacocks in Brinck's *Adversaria*, of many that exemplify the way in which knowledge was set in to place, much like the juxtaposition of items in collections of the time. The second feature of Brinck's *Adversaria* and of his collections that merits highlighting is the temporal shuffle of his recollections and observations. His garden, another sort of collection, is recalled in one of the notebooks, where he attempts to itemize its contents. The heading under which he does so is «Index omnis generis Florum», the extensive subheading of which reads:

> that are found in our lands [...] most of which I have had and many more others which have not survived because when my garden existed in the years 1608–9–10–11–12 I had over 300 sorts of plants, the names of some of which elude me.[48]

Brinck's text is motivated by an encyclopedic drive to list all of a kind, but gives way to the indomitable passage of time and the loss of memory. Order is only as good as its memory; this brief paragraph is redolent of the keen struggle to preserve and to structure a sea of particulars. Bacon recommended that

> whatsoever the hand of man by exquisite art or engine has made rare in stuff, form or motion; whatsoever singularity, chance, and the shuffle of things hath produced; whatsoever Nature hath wrought in things that want life and may be kept; shall be sorted and included.[49]

and in Brinck's compilations of data we encounter just that shuffle, sorted and included.

Annotations

1   The literature on the history of collecting is too extensive to cite more than summarily here: See principally Julius von Schlosser, *Die Kunst- und Wunderkammern der Spätrenaissance. Ein Beitrag zur Geschichte des Sammelwesens*, Leipzig 1908; Oliver Impey and Arthur Macgregor, eds., *The Origins of Museums. The Cabinet of Curiosities in Sixteenth- and Seventeenth-Century Europe*, London 2001; 1st ed. 1985; Adalgisa Lugli, *Naturalia et Mirabilia. Il collezionismo enciclopedico nelle Wunderkammern in Europa*, Milan 1983; Antoine Schnapper, *Le géant, la licorne, et la tulipe. Collections et collectionneurs dans la France du XVIIe siècle. I – Histoire et histoire naturelle*, Paris 1988; Joy Kenseth, ed., *The Age of the Marvelous*, exh. cat., Hanover, NH 1991; Ellinoor Bergvelt and Renée Kistenmaker, eds., *De wereld binnen handbereik. Nederlandse kunst- en rariteitenverzamelingen, 1585–1735*, 2 vols., exh. cat., Amsterdam 1992; Ellinoor Bergvelt et al., eds., *Verzamelen. Van rariteitenkabinet tot kunstmuseum*, Heerlen 2005; Thomas DaCosta Kaufmann, «From Mastery of the World to Mastery of Nature: The *Kunstkammer*, Politics, and Science», in: *The Mastery of Nature. Aspects of Art, Science, and Humanism in the Renaissance*, Princeton 1993, p. 174–194; Paula Findlen, *Possessing Nature. Museums, Collecting and Scientific Culture in Early Modern Italy*, Berkeley/Los Angeles/London, 1994; Lorraine Daston and Katharine Park, *Wonders and the Order of Nature 1150–1750*, New York 1998, esp. chapters IV and VII; Bob van den Boogert et al., *Rembrandt's Treasures*, exh. cat., Zwolle 1999; Eric Jorink, *Reading the Book of Nature in the Dutch Golden Age, 1575–1715*, Leiden 2010.

2   On Brinck, see F.A. van Rappard, *Ernst Brinck, eerste serctretaris van het Nederlandsche gezantschap te Konstantinopel...*, Utrecht 1868; Jorink 2010 (as note 1), p. 289–299 and 332; Henk Hovenkamp, *Ernst Brinck (1582–1649), een bijzondere Harderwijker*, Harderwijk 2012. I am deeply grateful to Dr. Jorink for encouraging me to study Brink further, and to Mr. Hovenkamp and the Streekarchivariaat Noordwest-Veluwe for having welcomed me. Brinck's oeuvre is multi-faceted and multi-lingual and, in its complexity, calls out for collaborative study. I could ask for no finer introduction to a long-term collaborative study than these two scholars have so generously offered. I would also like to thank Jaap van der Veen for very fruitful conversations and generous feedback.

3   Language is a formidable barrier, and there is excellent literature in Dutch—much of it, as explained shortly, focusing on later seventeenth-century developments. See, for example, Bergvelt and Kistenmaker 1992 (as note 1); Jaap van der Veen, «De verzamelaar in zijn kamer. Zeventiende-eeuwse privé-collecties in de Republiek», in: *Ons soort mensen. Levensstijlen in Nederland*, ed. by H. de Jonge, Nijmegen 1997, p. 125–158; *Schatten in Delft. Burgers verzamelen 1600–1750*, ed. by Ellinoor Bergvelt et al., Zwolle 2002. Notable recent exceptions to the tendency to publish studies of Dutch collecting in Dutch (only) include Jorink 2010 (as note 1) and, though not strictly about collecting, Florike Egmond, *The World of Carolus* Clusius: *Natural History in the Making, 1550–1610*, London 2010.

4   On Dutch collecting in general, see further Roelof van Gelder, «De wereld binnen handbereik. Nederlandse kunst- en rariteitenverzamelingen, 1585–1735», in: Bergvelt and Kistemaker 1992 (as note 1), p. 15–38. On the collection housed in the gallery of the Leiden University hortus, see Erik de Jong, *Nature and Art. Dutch Garden and Landscape Architecture, 1650–1740*, Philadelphia 2001, esp. p. 136–157.

5   David Freedberg, «Science, Commerce, and Art. Neglected Topics at the Junction of History and Art History», in: *Art in history. History in art*, ed. by David Freedberg and J. de Vries, Santa Monica 1991, p. 377–428; J. Driessen, *Tsaar Peter de Grote en zijn Amsterdamse vrienden*, Amsterdam 1996; J.J. Driessen-van het Reve, *De Kunstkamera van Peter de Grote. De Hollandse inbreng, gereconstrueerd uit brieven van Albert Seba en Johann Daniel Schumacher uit de jaren 1711–1752*, Amsterdam 2006; Daniel Margocsy, «A Museum of Wonders or a Cemetery of Corpses? The Commercial Exchange of Anatomical Collections in Early Modern Netherlands», in:, *Silent Messengers. The Circulation of Material Objects of Knowledge in the Early Modern Low Countries*, de. by Sven Dupré and Christoph Lüthy, Berlin 2011, p. 185–215. On Witsen, see Marion Peters, *De wijze koopman. Het wereldwijde onderzoek van Nicolaes Witsen (1641–1717), burgemeester en VOC-bewindhebber van Amsterdam*, Amsterdam 2010.

6   Francis Bacon, *Gesta Grayorum*, London 1688, p. 35.

7   Jorink 2010 (as note 1). See also Egmond 2010 (as note 3).

8   J.A. Worp, *De briefwisseling van Constantijn Huygens, 1608–1687*, 6 vols., The Hague 1911–1917, vol. 1, nr. 482, p. 272–273, 1 January 1630 to Caspar Barlaeus.

9   Index Rervm Omnivm Natvralivm, a Bernhardo Palvdano, Medicinæ Doctore, et Civitatis Enckhvsensis Physico experientissimo, collectarum, in: *Warhaffte Beschreibung Zweyer Raisen*, Tübingen 1603; F.W.T. Hunger, «Bernardus Paludanus (Berent ten Broecke) 1550–1633. Zijn verzamelingen en zijn werk», in: *Itinerario*

17

voyage ofte schipvaert van Jan Huygen van Linschoten naer oost ofte Portugaels Indien 1579–1592, ed. by H. Kern, 8 vols., The Hague, 1910–1957, vol. 3, p. 249–268; Marie-Christine Engels, «Een combinatie van Kunst en Wetenschap: de verzameling van Bernardus Paludanus (1550–1633)», in: *Steevast* (Jaarboek van de Vereniging Oud Enkhuizen) 1997, p. 32–36; Roelof van Gelder, «Paradijsvogels in Enkhuizen. De relatie tussen Van Linschoten en Bernardus Paludanus», in: *Souffrir pour Parvenir. De wereld van Jan Huygen van Linschoten*, ed. by Roelof van Gelder, Jan Parmentier and Vibeke Roeper, Haarlem 1998, p. 30–50; Florike Egmond, «Een mislukte benoeming. Paludanus en de Leidse universiteit», in: ibid., p. 51–64; Harold J. Cook, *Matters of Exchange. Commerce, Medicine, and Science in the Dutch Golden Age*, New Haven and London 2007, esp. Chapter 2, «Reformations Tempered: In Pursuit of Natural Facts», p. 82–132; and, most recently, Jorink 2010 (as note 1), esp. p. 266–278.

10 The religious articles listed in the 1617 inventory of Paludanus's collection are cited by Jorink 2010 (as note 1), p. 272–273.

11 Raphael Pelecius to Caspar Bauhin, 20 Aug. 1594 (Basel UB, MS. Fr.Gr. II.1, p. 42, IV), as cited and transl. by Brian Ogilvie, *The Science of Describing. Natural History in Renaissance Europe*, Chicago 2006, p. 41.

12 «Ad Paludanum de ejus Admirandis», Hug. Grotius, *Poemata Omnia*, Leiden 1645, p. 232–233.

13 Claudia Swan, «Making Sense of Medical Collections in Early Modern Holland: The Uses of Wonder», in *Knowledge and its Making in Early Modern Europe*, ed. by Pamela H. Smith and Benjamin Schmidt, Chicago 2007, p. 199–213.

14 «Sonderling-Heden oft Rariteyten ende Wtgelesen Sinnelickheden/ Van Indiaensche ende andere wtheemsche Zee-horens/ Schelpen/ Eerd ende Zeegewassen/ Mineralen/ ende oock vreemde Gedierten; mitsgaders eeinighe constichlijck ghemaecte handwercken ende schilderijen/ Die Christiaen Porret, wijlen Apoteker/ in zijn Cunstcamer vergadert had». See Swan 2007 (as note 13), p. 199–213. Oddly, Porret does not figure in Jorink 2010 (as note 1). One copy survives in the RKD in The Hague and another in Dresden. See Frits Lugt, *Répertoire des Catalogues de Ventes Publiques Intéressant l'Art ou la Curiosité. Première Période vers 1600–1825*, The Hague 1938, no. 2; E.W. Moes, «De sonderling-heden oft rariteyten ende wtgelesen sinnelickheden van Christiaen Porret», in: Leids Jaarboekje, 1905, vol. II, p. 93–100; introduces the collection and the collector; other biographical information is to be found in Henriëtte A. Bosman-Jelgersma, «De lotgevallen van een apothekersleerling in het 17de-eeuwse Leiden», in: *Leids Jaarboekje*, 1987, vol. LXXIX, p. 62–81.

15 «De Heer Ernst Brinck in leven Burgemeester deser stadt en een groot onderzoeker van outheden, wiens gedachtenis om sijn sonderlinge geleertheit van verscheiden talen, en desselfs Konstcamer en andere curiositeiten hier na sal gedaght werden, bekent in sijne aentekeningen over Harderwijck». Hovenkamp 2012 (as note 2), p. 3.

16 Van Rappard 1868 (as note 2); Hovenkamp 2012 (as note 2).

17 Koninklijke Bibliotheek, The Hague, 133 M 86, 135 K 4, 133 M 87, (KB).

18 KB 135 K 4, fol. 63r. Galilei's entry states: «An: 1614. D.19 Novembris | Ut Nobili, ac generoso studio | D: Ernesti Brinckii rem grata | facerem Galileus Galilei Flo- | rentius manu propria scripti | Florentie». See *The Origins of the Telescope*, ed. by Albert van Helden, Sven Dupré, Rob van Gent, and Huib Zuidervaart, Amsterdam 2011, fn. 1.

19 Streekarchivariaat Noordwest-Veluwe, archief stadsbestuur Harderwijk 1231–1813 (OAH), in.nrs. 2013–2061, *Adversaria van Dr. Ernst Brinck*, 46 volumes and 3 portfolios, (OAH).

20 Ann M. Blair, *Too Much to Know. Managing Scholarly Information before the Modern Age*, New Haven and London 2010, p. 76.

21 Ibid., p. 87.

22 Cited in Anthony Grafton and Joanna Weinberg, ‹I have always loved the Holy Tongue›. *Isaac Casaubon, the Jews, and a Forgotten Chapter in Renaissance Scholarship*, Cambridge MA 2011, p. 15, fn. 57. Over 60 books of *Adversaria* by Isaac Casaubon are in the collection of the Bodleian Library, Oxford.

23 Blair 2010 (as note 20), p. 78, citing Jeremias Drexel, SJ, *Aurifodina atrium et scientiarum omnium; excerpendi sollertia*, Antwerp 1638.

24 OAH nr. 2038, fol. 6r-v, fol. 23r, fol. 57r-v; OAH nr. 2037, fol. 46r.

25 Blair 2010 (as note 20), p. 64.

26 OAH nr. 2024a. See J.A.J. Barge, *De oudste inventaris der oudste academische anatomie in Nederland*, Leiden 1934; Henricus Cramer, A catalogue of all the cheifest rarities in the publick theater and anatomie…, Leiden 1727. The objects listed by Brinck correspond by and large with those «In the great Cupboard L on the South-side of the Anatomie», p. 11–13.

27 In addition to Blair 2010 (as note 20) see Alberto Cevolini, *De arte excerpendi. Imparare a dimenticare nella modernità*, Florence 2006, with Italian translations of sections of key texts (Sacchini, Drexler, etc.); Jean-Marc Chatelain, «Humanisme et culture de la note», in: *Revue de la Bibliothèque nationale de France*, 1999, Bd. 2, p. 26–36.

28 Deborah E. Harkness, «Accounting for

Science. How a Merchant Kept his Books in Elizabethan London», in: *The Self-Perception of Early Modern Capitalists*, ed. by Margaret C. Jacob and Catherine Secretan, New York 2008, p. 205–229, at p. 205.

29 KB 135 K 4, fols. 81, 121; see also 144–145; notations on sign language of the Seraglio begin at fol. 184; cf. OAH 2046, fol. 45r.; see also Jorink 2010 (as note 1), fig. 49.

30 Jorink 2010 (as note 1), p. 290; on the location of Dutch collections within homes, see van der Veen 1997 (as note 2).

31 Brinck's album KB 133 M 86, fol. 199r contains an inscription by Bernardus Paludanus dated 26 May 1610. To the best of my knowledge, Brinck did not sign Paludanus's album; the latter is preserved in the Koninklijke Bibliotheek (133 M 63) and contains upwards of 1900 signatures. See also Louise E. van Wijk, «Het album amicorum van Bernardus Paludanus», in: *Het Boek* 1948, 29, p. 265–286.

32 I am deeply grateful to Henk Hovenkamp for sharing his transcriptions of passages from Brinck's *Adversaria* and albums, organized chronologically.

33 Imperato's signature is found at KB 135 K 4, fol. 61r; the notes on birds are in OAH 2057, fol. 154r.

34 «Anno 1614 heb ick te Romen in het Cabinett vanden Paus Paulo .V. gesien een struijss eij, op het welcke seer constich gesneden was die Passie Christi; Item noch een ander op het welcke gegraviert was, een Angus Dei, seer aerdich». OAH 2057, fol. 5v.

35 OAH 2058, fol. 8r. He uses the term ‹musaeum› elsewhere, as for example with reference to Pieter Pauw in Leiden at OAH 2057, fol. 14r («Pica Indica»). This may be a reference to the Leiden anatomical theater or to the botanical garden.

36 «Te Pratelino (Pratolino). 5. mijlen van Florentz gelegen, heb ick A° 1614 oeck met geneuchten besichtiget, het wijtvermaerde Lusthuijss des Groothartogen aldaer, twelck is een seer voortreffelijck Palatium, alwaer te sien sijn schone lusthoven, fontijnen, ende veel wonderbaerlicke antiquiteijten ende rariteijten [...] voor all is daer waerdich om sijn, het Aviarium [...] door dit vogelhuijss loopt oeck een klein beecksgen, is veel konstiger ende natuijrlicker, als dat tot Fontainebelleau, het welcke naer dit schijnt gemaeckt te sijn; Dit te Pratelino, is 40 treden lanck, is boven over heen met ijserdraet ende tralikens toegemaeckt, daerin bevinden haer etlicke duijsent vogelen van allerleij soorten». OAH 2057, fol. 173v.

37 «In het vogelhuijss van Prints Maurits, in den Haghe, heb ick Anno 21. gesien, en gants witten exter, hebbende oeck een witten beck, was uuijt Brabandt gekomen; was in een kouwe apart. Aldaer heb ick doenmaels oeck gesien in een kouwe een grauwen exter». OAH 2057, fol. 77. On the phoenix, see fol. 16r.

38 For example, shells in the West India Company headquarters at OAH 2059, fol. 82r. «In de Rustcamer van der Churvorst van Saxen te Dresden; in een bijsondere camer wierden mij Anno 15 vertoont, allerleij vederbosschen, soo van swaerte als witte Reijgers, waeronder dat was een bosch van swarte Reijgers vederen geestimeert op .5000. daelders, den welcken van Keijser Rodolphs .2. vereert was anden Churvorst». OAH 2057, fol. 123r. At OAH fol. 15v, Brinck mentions seeing ten birds of paradise together, in the same collection.

39 OAH 2057, fol. 15r. In Dutch, «Bij ...», «Wickefoort» in Amsterdam is likely the diplomat Joachim Wickefort/Wicquefort (1596–1660), whose correspondence with Caspar Barlaeus was published.

40 A portfolio containing loose leaves, OAH 2061. The poem is by Nicolaus Heinsius and in Latin. The portfolio contains another poem on the collection, in Dutch, by G. Caroli (?).

41 OAH 2057, fol. 2v.

42 OAH 2057, fol. 5v.

43 OAH 2057, fol. 15v.

44 OAH 2057, fol. 27r. These could not have been preserved from his own eagle, which died in 1637. Brinck states that he had had this eagle for ten years. See OAH 2057, fol. 26v.

45 OAH 2057, fol. 14v. See also Jorink 2010 (as note 1), p. 291.

46 OAH 2057, fol. 71r.

47 OAH 2057, fol. 43r. The featherwork image of *The Mass of St. Gregory* (Musée de Jacobins, Auch, France), ca. 1539 is the oldest-known surviving colonial work of its kind; it was presented as a gift to Pope Paul III.

48 «Index ois. generis florum diemen in dese onse Contreijen is hebbende dese naegespecificeerde heb ick meist alle gehadt, ende noch veel meer anderen die vergaen sijn want doen mijn Hortus Floridum anno .1608.9.10.11.12 noch in esse was, soo heb ick daerin bevonden over de 300 verscheiden soorten van bloemen, waer van sommiger namen mij ontgaen sijn». OAH 2033, fol. 70r.

49 See above, note 6.

Robert Felfe
Naturabgüsse – künstliche Zeugung und Kreisläufe des Lebens

Ungeachtet der Verluste und teils irreversiblen Beschädigungen hat allein die Sockelzone des so genannten *Merkelschen Tafelaufsatzes* nichts von jener Faszination verloren, die allein zu beschreiben, eine Herausforderung ist. Zahlreiche Abgüsse nach der Natur lassen hier eine Mikrolandschaft von verblüffender Lebendigkeit erstehen, obwohl die Differenzen zu den natürlichen Dingen offensichtlich sind. Die silbrigen Körper winziger Eidechsen – es wurden hier tatsächlich Jungtiere abgeformt – bevölkern zusammen mit kleinen Krebsen, Heuschrecken und Feuerwanzen ein überraschend vielgestaltiges Gelände.[1] Ebenfalls abgegossene Kräuter, Blüten und einzelne Blätter an ihren Stängeln bedecken Mulden und Böschungen als veritables Dickicht. Zwar hat jedes Detail an sich zwangsläufig seine natürliche Größe, und doch widersprechen sie einander in der Kombination. Die künstliche Landschaft mit ihren amorphen Bodenformationen, *animalia* und *vegetabilia* ist zugleich von suggestiver Ähnlichkeit zu den Naturdingen und erscheint extrem fremd. – Alle Vegetation schießt auf kurzem Weg zu Blüten und Samenkapseln auf und suggeriert im Unterholz bereits die Konturen von Bäumen und ganzen Wäldern. Unter dem Blätterdach hauchdünn metallener Kräuter führen die Tiere eine eigene, in ihrer Selbstgenügsamkeit undurchdringliche Existenz.

Allein diese Eindrücke legen es nahe, der Praxis frühneuzeitlicher Naturabgüsse erneut nachzugehen. Der Impuls dazu rührt aus der Vermutung, dass so unumstößlich erscheinende Kategorien wie die von ‹Kunst› und ‹Natur› in Hinblick auf diese Kunstwerke in ihrem Zusammenhang neu zu denken sind. – Die bisherige Forschung hat eine Reihe markanter Momente dieser Kleinplastiken eingehend diskutiert. Gleichwohl bergen sie nach wie vor Probleme und offene Fragen. Gingen frühe Studien vor allem dem Phänomen eines ‹Naturalismus› der Renaissance nach,[2] so rührten daraus Impulse, der spezifischen Ästhtetik dieser Kleinplastiken und deren psychologischen Implikationen nachzugehen.[3] Vor allem in jüngerer Zeit wurden sowohl Abgussverfahren[4] wie auch die Frage nach dem Verhältnis von Kunst und Natur erneut und unter neuen Prämissen diskutiert. Im Zentrum stand dabei nicht mehr die Frage, ob sich in diesen Bildwerken ein ‹Naturalismus› artikuliere, der den Kunstcharakter dieser Werke zu negieren versucht habe. Vielmehr wurde nun verfolgt, welche Konzepte von Natur dieser Kunst zugrunde lagen und inwiefern sie zugleich naturkundliche Wissenspraxis war.[5]

Die folgenden Überlegungen fühlen sich insbesondere diesen neueren Ansätzen verbunden – zugleich aber versuchen sie ein Desiderat dieser Arbeiten einzulösen. Eine bloße Parallelführung von naturkundlichem Wissen, kunsthandwerklicher Praxis und ikonologischer Deutung der Werke reicht nicht aus, um die tatsächliche Relevanz dieser Artefakte zu erfassen. Die zentrale These ist daher, dass die plastischen Bilder metallener Abgüsse nach der Natur zugleich als natürliche wie auch künstliche und damit auf einzigartige Weise lebendige Körper geschaffen und verstanden wurden. Diese Sinndimension rührte aus der Technologie des Abguss' und in ihr waren wiederum ikonografische Schichten dieser Kleinplastiken verankert.

Kunckels Rezepte – Naturabguss als ‹substitutiver Bildakt›[6]
An Umfang und Detailfülle selten reiche Quellen zu Verfahren des Abgießens nach der Natur stammen aus der zweiten Hälfte des 17. Jahrhunderts und gehen auf Johann Kunckel zurück.[7] Als Chemiker, Apotheker, Glasmacher und Metallurg stand Kunckel im Dienst der Kurfürsten von Sachsen und Brandenburg; Ende des 17. Jahrhunderts gehörte ihm die Pfaueninsel bei Berlin, wo er ein eigenes Laboratorium insbesondere zur Glasherstellung betrieb.[8] In der *Curieusen Kunst- und Werck-Schul* von 1696 werden auf nicht weniger als 50 Seiten eine Reihe verschiedener Abgusstechniken nach der Natur vorgestellt.[9] Gegossen wird in verschiedenen Metallen und Gips, in kompakten einteiligen wie auch in mehrteiligen Formen, massiv oder mit Hohlkern. Sujets sind sowohl Pflanzen, Insekten, Schlangen, Frösche, Eidechsen und andere Tiere – bis hin zum lebenden Menschen.[10] Angesichts der jeweils komplexen Abläufe weisen wiederkehrende Momente auffällige Überlagerungen von technologisch bedingtem Arbeitsschritt und symbolischer Handlung auf. Auf diese Weise werden beide als unlösbar miteinander verwobene Aspekte desselben Prozesses dargestellt.

Die meisten Gussverfahren verlangen, dass das ursprüngliche Lebewesen die Prozedur nicht überlebt. Insbesondere Tiere sind zu töten, um zu verhindern, dass sie durch Eigenbewegungen das Aushärten der Form stören. Zudem könnte es sein, dass man einzelne Tierkörper im Sinne eines ganz bestimmten Arrangements fixieren möchte. Schlangen, Eidechsen oder auch Insekten sind mithin in der Regel zu töten, *bevor* der eigentliche Abformungsprozess beginnt. Hierzu wird empfohlen, sie in Wein, Essig oder Branntwein zu «ertränken», wobei wiederum bei Essig die Gefahr groß sei, dass die Oberfläche der Tiere angegriffen oder gar zerstört werde.[11]

Es ist ein wiederkehrendes Moment in Kunckels Schilderungen, dass die lebenden Wesen nicht nur sterben müssen, sondern dass deren Tod geradezu zelebriert wird. Gleich im ersten der beschriebenen Verfahren werden die abzugießenden Teile von Pflanzen in eigens hergestellte Kästchen gelegt, die in etwa ihrer Größe entsprechen und sie bequem aufnehmen. Diese hölzernen Kästchen werden als «Zärglein» oder «Särglein» bezeichnet.[12] Die abzugießenden Objekte werden somit zu Beginn in kleinen Sarkophagen bestattet und mit der Gussmasse gleichsam beerdigt.

Herbeigeführter Tod und Bestattung sind dabei weit mehr als entweder rein technologische Notwendigkeit oder bloß metaphorische Rede. Dies wird in einem der nächsten Schritte deutlich, der mit geringen Abweichungen in allen Verfahren fast identisch ist. Nach dem Erhärten der Negativform muss der Körper von Tieren und Pflanzen für den bevorstehenden Guss zerstört und restlos aus der Form entfernt werden. Mit einigen Varianten im Detail der Ausführung wird diese Vernichtung durch Hitzeeinwirkung, das heißt durch Feuer herbeigeführt. Die erwähnten «Särglein» zum Beispiel sollen nach einer Weile mit kalten und dann mit glühenden Kohlen bedeckt werden «damit die Hitze von oben hinab wohl erglühe und schmelze».[13] Mitunter wird hierbei vom «Ausglühen» oder vom «Ausbrennen» der einst lebenden Körper gesprochen.[14] Bei diesem Vorgang wird einerseits die Form für den bevorstehenden Metallguss gehärtet. Zugleich aber geht es dezidert um die restlose Tilgung der alten materiellen Existenz von Pflanzen oder Tieren. In einer der für Tiere vorgeschlagenen Techniken des Abgusses in einem «Rohr» oder «Geschirr» wird die komplette Zerstörung des Tierkörpers explizit als Pulverisierung beschrieben. Es heißt hier: «und brenne das Thier / so in Leimen [dem Material der Gussform] ist / heraus zu Pulver».[15] In einem weiteren, vorrangig für Pflanzen empfohlenen Verfahren heißt es: «wann er [der Gips der herzustellenden Form] nun wohl trocken / und ohn einige Feuchtigkeit ist / müsset ihr ihn wohl ausglühen / damit die Blume inwendig / sich ganz verzehre».[16]

Die verbliebenen Überreste des von Hitze zerstörten alten Körpers müssen daraufhin akribisch entfernt werden und dies ist zugleich der Moment, in dem die in der Gussform aufgefangene Gestalt des Lebewesens für eine erneute Formgebung freigelegt wird. Insbesondere bei einteiligen Gussformen kann dies schwierig werden, und auch hierfür empfiehlt der Autor verschiedene Verfahren, in denen erneut technischer Ablauf und symbolische Handlungen miteinander verschränkt sind. Zur unmittelbaren Vorbereitung der Gussform wird mehrfach empfohlen, die verbliebene Asche der Naturalien mit dem Atem heraus zu ziehen. Der eigene Atem reinigt dabei die Form wobei der ausführende Künstler sich unweigerlich mindestens Teile der stofflichen Überreste seiner Objekte einverleibt.[17] Außerdem kann diese abschließende Reinigung der Form vor dem Guss auch durch Quecksilber geschehen: «Und damit alles heraus kommt / und die Form rein gesäubert werde / so lässet man ein wenig Quecksilber darein lauffen / das suchet alles heraus / so noch etwas darinnen stecken blieben.»[18]

Auch dieser Arbeitsschritt ist weit mehr als die bloße Umsetzung technologischer Notwendigkeiten. Sicher, die Form muss für einen qualitätvollen Guss frei von Asche und sonstigen Überresten sein. Hier aber wird die Reinigung – zwischen der Vernichtung des toten, alten Körpers und der Entstehung eines neuen – als Vorgang beschrieben, bei dem der Künstler die negative Form des potentiellen Bildwerks im wahrsten Sinne beatmet oder von Quecksilber durchströmen lässt. Diese Verwendung des Quecksilbers scheint sich nicht nur aus dem allgemein hohen Rang dieses Metalls in der Alchemie herzuleiten – als ‹lebendiges Silber› eine äußerst subtile Substanz und zugleich philosophisches Prinzip stofflicher Wandlungen.[19] Sie ruft hier den antiken Ingenieur Daidalos in Erinnerung, der – wie Aristoteles berichtet – die Athener in großes Erstaunen über eine Staue der Aphrodite versetzte, indem er Quecksilber in die verborgenen Innenräume der Plastik füllte woraufhin diese sich von selbst bewegt habe.[20]

Im darauf folgenden Schritt – dem eigentlichen Guss – materialisiert sich die Gestalt der natürlichen Wesen aufs Neue, dieses mal in Metall. Eingehend werden hierfür die jeweils herzustellenden Legierungen, die Anlage der Gusskanäle und zu verwendende Flussmittel beschrieben. Dies sind die letzten Schritte vor dem Guss selbst, mit dem der Formprozess zum Abschluss kommt.

In diesem technischen Ablauf realisieren sich Tötung und Zerstörung der natürlichen Wesen somit als Bedingung und notwendige Schritte zur Genese eines neuen Körpers. Dessen Herstellung zielt auf einen neuen, dem Lebendigen verwandten Status dieser Artefakte und diese Lebendigkeit ist kein bloß kunsttheoretisches Postulat. Die faktische Durchdringung des technologischen Prozesses mit Vorgängen der Tötung und plastischen Substitution findet ihren Ausdruck etwa in den Beschreibungen eines Verfahrens, das als besonders subtil empfohlen wird, da es mit ihm möglich sei, verschiedenste Tiere und Pflanzen abzugießen, «als wann sie natürlich allso gewachsen wären».[21]

Zum einen beschreiben Formulierungen wie diese eine *ästhetische Wirkung* der fertigen Werke, die das Urteilsvermögen eines Betrachters herausfordert. In Hinblick auf dasselbe Verfahren wird dem Leser nämlich versprochen: «so werdet ihr eine Eyder haben / die von einer natürlichen gar nicht zu unterscheiden» ist.[22] Es ist diese lebensechte Erscheinung von Naturabgüssen als ästhetische Qualität forcierter Ähnlichkeit, die selbst Vasari in Hinblick auf die Metallabgüsse von Pflanzen ausdrücklich als eine Kunst würdigte, in der die zeitgenössischen Meister die Alten übertroffen hätten.[23]

Das Auge war jedoch nicht der alleinige Adressat dieser Kunstwerke. Bereits 1547 hatte der Nürnberger Schreib- und Rechenmeister Johann Neudörfer in seinen *Nachrichten von Künstlern und Werkleuten* unter den vielfältigen Werken und Fähigkeiten der Gebrüder Wenzel und Albrecht Jamnitzer insbesondere deren Naturabgüsse hervorgehoben. Die in Silber gegossenen «Thierlein, Würmlein, Kräuter und Schnecken» werden hier als beispiellos gepriesen. Seinen Höhepunkt findet der Eintrag zu den Jamnitzers jedoch speziell mit den Abgüssen von Pflanzen, deren «Blättlein und Kräutlein also subtil und dünn sind, dass sie auch ein Anblasen wehig macht».[24]

Freilich gehört diese Passage zu den unermüdlich in der Forschung zitierten Quellen. In diesem beeindruckenden Detail steckt jedoch weit mehr als der bloße Hinweis darauf, dass diese künstlichen *vegetabilia* an Subtilität den natürlichen Pflanzen nahe kommen. Sie tun dies, indem sie auf den menschlichen Atem reagieren. Sie verhalten sich wie lebendige Pflanzen und in ihrer Bewegung findet noch einmal jener menschliche Atemwind ein Echo, der bereits am Gussvorgang beteiligt war. Weil sie auf diese Weise leben, beeilt sich der Autor unmittelbar im Anschluss zu versichern, dass die Künstler aber für diese besonderen Fähigkeiten Gott allein die Ehre geben. Diese für Neudörfers Nachrichten sehr untypische fromme Ehrerbietung ist in dieser Form nur als Demutsbekundung zu verstehen. Ausgesprochen wird sie, gerade weil die Goldschmiede in ihrer Kunst auf einem Terrain arbeiten, das eigentlich dem göttlichen Schöpfer vorbehalten ist.

Wenn der visuelle Eindruck von Naturabgüssen gelegentlich beschrieben wurde «als wenn sie natürlich also gewachsen wären»,[25] dann meint dies nicht allein die verblüffende Ähnlichkeit und den ‹response› des fertigen Kunstwerks. Die skizzierte Durchdringung des technologischen Prozesses mit hochgradig symbolisch aufgeladenen Operationen wird in einigen Varianten der Gusstechnologie nochmals zugespitzt und überboten. Dabei wird deutlich, inwiefern Begriffe und Konzepte abbildender Repräsentation die Genese und den Status dieser Bildwerke grundsätzlich verfehlen.

Es ist nämlich keineswegs unausweichlich, das abzugießende Tier *apriori* zu töten. Dies gilt zum einen für schwache Tiere, vornehmlich Insekten, die für die Abnahme der Form lebendig fixiert werden können: «…was aber gar schwach ist / kanst du wohl mit Terpentin lebendig aufhefften / darnach geuß den Zeug [tonähnliches Material der künftigen Gussform] darüber / wie sonsten.»[26] Zum anderen wird eine ziemlich brachiale Methode geschildert: «Wie man ein lebendiges / fliegendes / oder sonst dergleichen Thier / als Vögel / Frösch / Eydern und anders in eine Formen gießen und drucken kann.»[27] Dabei wird das Tier lebendig in ein verschließbares «Geschirr» oder «Rohr» gesperrt und in dieses Gefäß wird sodann die flüssige Masse der künftigen Gussform eingefüllt. Bevor das Material erhärtet, müsse man dabei Holzstäbchen oder ähnliches, von außen an den Körper des Tieres heranführen und in dieser Position fixieren, um so die späteren Gusskanäle zu erhalten.

In den beiden letztgenannten Verfahren stirbt das Tier erst in der erstarrenden Gussform. Das heißt: Sein Leben geht im Inneren des irdenen Materials unmittelbar in die Ausbildung jener Negativform über, in der später das eigentliche Werk entstehen wird. Noch direkter als wenn das Tier zuvor getötet wird, kommt es in diesen Verfahren zum unmittelbaren Kontakt von lebendigem Wesen und Bildform. Lebendes Wesen und Bildkörper werden zeitlich direkt miteinander gekoppelt. Diese temporale Verkettung ist *ein* Moment, aufgrund dessen das Bildwerk als Substitut im strengen Sinne eines Nachfolgers des lebenden Wesens anzusprechen ist.

Prägnanter als bei anderen Verfahren wird zudem hier, beim Abgießen lebender Tiere, der Metallguss selbst geschildert, als handle es sich dabei um die quasi selbstständige Annahme einer Form durch eine dafür geeignete Materie. Wenn die Form abgenommen und das verendete Tier pulverisiert und entfernt ist, dann – so heißt es recht lapidar – «geuß ein Metall / was dich gelust so gewinnet es dessen Gestalt».[28] Der ästhetische Eindruck von Abgüssen – als wären sie so «gewachsen» – wird in dieser Formulierung gusstechnisch hinterfüttert. Die suggestive Ähnlichkeit der fertigen Bildwerke, so legt diese Passage nahe, ist der Effekt eines Prozesses, in dem die Kunst eine formbildende Selbstorganisation von Materie initiiert.

Es geht bei den Naturabgüssen somit *nicht* um ein bildnerisches Verfahren, bei dem *dort* ein bestimmtes Sujet existiert, dass *hier* im Werk dargestellt wird. Der Gussvorgang nach der verlorenen Form ist vielmehr dezidiert als eine Transformation verstanden worden, in deren Verlauf der Körper des Tieres in den des Bildwerkes überführt wird.

Kunst als ‹Spontanzeugung›
Als was aber lassen sich dann die metallenen Bildkörper der Abgüsse verstehen? – In der genannten Quelle kommt den ausgiebig beschriebenen Gussverfahren zugleich eine signifikante Position im Rahmen einer umfassenden Ordnung der Künste und Praktiken zu. Sie stehen zwischen den vorangehenden Ausführungen zur Metallbearbeitung und einem Kapitel, das unter der Überschrift «Allerhand schöne und rare Curiositäten» sich tatsächlich mit der Hervorbringung von Lebewesen beschäftigt.[29] Es beginnt mit einem Versuch zur «regeneratio plantarum». Dabei werden die Samen von einem beliebigen Kraut zunächst gemahlen, daraus eine wässrige Lösung angesetzt, aus der wiederum über Wochen oder gar Monate erneut das entsprechende Kraut hervorgehe. Bereits im dritten Versuch wird «Ein schönes Silber-Gewächs» beschrieben,[30] und es folgen weitere Experimente, bei denen in geschlossenen Gefäßen aus Lösungen von Metallen, anderen Mineralien oder auch pflanzlichen Substanzen in einem Wachstumsprozess florale Formen entstehen. Unter einer Vielzahl derartiger «Kunststücklein» wird, analog zu den Pflanzen, schließlich auch «Von der Regeneration der Thiere» berichtet.[31] Das Spektrum dieser Tiere deckt sich dabei auf markante Weise mit jenen Kleintieren, die bevorzugt abgegossen wurden. Dies gilt insbesondere für Krebse, Krö-

ten, Aale, Schlangen, Mäuse, Käfer und kleine Fische. Dabei ist es vor allem ein bestimmtes Prinzip (re)generativer Prozesse, auf das der Autor den Leser aufmerksam macht. All diese Tiere seien nämlich in der Lage, sich ohne geschlechtliche Zeugung – durch die so genannte ‹Spontanzeugung› – fortzupflanzen. Hierzu werden sowohl einzelne Naturphänomene als auch entsprechende Versuche detailliert beschrieben. Bei letzteren wird zunächst der Körper der jeweiligen Tiere komplett zerstört, d.h. pulverisiert oder verbrannt, bevor aus diesen formlosen Resten neue Tiere entstehen.

Diese vermeintlich ungeschlechtlichen Formen der Regenerationen haben eine lange Tradition in der naturphilosophischen bzw. -geschichtlichen Literatur.[32] In ihrer Breite lässt sie sich hier nicht wiedergeben – mit Aristoteles, Plinius, Giambattista della Porta, Ulisse Aldrovandi und Athansius Kircher seien lediglich die von Kunckel explizit vermerkten Protagonisten erwähnt.[33]

Die in diesem Zusammenhang für die Frühe Neuzeit grundlegende Referenz war Aristoteles – insbesondere dessen *Historia animalium* und *De generatione animalium*.[34] Im Druck lagen Übersetzungen von Theodore Gaza (1476) und von Joseph Cesar Scaliger (1619) vor.[35] Die Spontanzeugung wird in der aristotelischen Zoologie prinzipiell als eine von lediglich zwei in der Natur zu findenden Modi der Zeugung behandelt. Dabei unterscheiden sich Lebewesen, die sich durch Spontanzeugung fortpflanzen, grundsätzlich von jenen, bei denen die Nachkommen aus zweigeschlechtlicher Zeugung mit anschließender Entwicklungs- bzw. Wachstumsphase im Ei entstehen, wie es bei den meisten Blut durchströmten Lebewesen, d.h. den meisten Fischen, den Vögeln, vierbeinigen Landtieren und dem Menschen der Fall ist. Anders ist es bei den ‹spontan› Zeugenden. Hier nämlich rührt der formbildende Impuls aus einem einzelnen Körper, statt aus dem männlichen Samen, in Folge geschlechtlicher Paarung. Die weitere Entfaltung der Nachkommen wird vor allem als ein Reifeprozess geschildert; als vorrangige Orte dieser Art von Zeugung galten das Innere der Erde, schlammige Gewässer und das Meer.[36]

Die Einbettung der Abgüsse in Kunckels Kompendium menschlicher Künste und Gewerke – zwischen angewandter Metallurgie und der experimentellen Erzeugung von Leben – ist höchst signifikant. Zunächst präzisiert sie bekannte Verbindungen zwischen Naturabguss, Spontanzeugung und Alchemie, wie sie etwa für Bernard Palissy und seine *rustique figulines* bereits aufgezeigt wurden.[37] Dabei ist es jedoch nicht die alchemistische Prägung an sich, die es hier hervorzuheben gilt. Bis weit ins 17. Jahrhundert waren insbesondere die Metallurgie und ihre Techniken ein Kernbereich alchemistischen Naturwissens und von diesem kaum zu trennen.[38] So ist es nicht überraschend, *dass* etwa Walter Ryff 1547 für das Bildgießen einen gewissen «verstandt der naturlichen Alchimi» dringend empfahl.[39] Wenn er aber inmitten der allgemeinen Ausführungen zu Legierungen, Schmelzvorgängen und zur Formherstellung als konkrete Sujets ausschließlich «Schlenglin / Eyderen / Heuschrecken und dergleichen gewürm / wie auch Blümlin / früchtlin unnd dergleichen» erwähnt, dann scheint es, als stünden diese Naturabgüsse gleichsam prototypisch für die Überführung von extrem wandelbarer Materie in Prozesse bildnerischer Formgebung.[40]

Die suggestive Wirkung von Naturabgüssen – als wären sie lebendig – war für Ryff, wie auch 150 Jahre später für Kunckel offenbar kein ästhetischer Selbstzweck. Die seit Pliuns vielfach überlieferte besonders zwingende Ähnlichkeit zwischen Bildwerk und Sujet ist nur ein Aspekt der Wertschätzung dieser Bildwerke.⁴¹ Vielmehr wurde der suggestive Eindruck von Lebendigkeit als Effekt eines technischen Prozedere gesehen, das seinerseits eine bestimmte Form der Generation von Leben imitierte. Vermutlich ist dies eine einmalige Konstellation in der Geschichte der Kunst: Kunsttechnologischer Prozess und sinnlich wahrnehmbare Erscheinung der Werke entsprechen sich vollkommen in der Weise, dass sie komplementär einen Anspruch auf Lebendigkeit erfüllen. Gelungene Abgüsse sehen nicht nur lebenden Tieren verblüffend ähnlich, sondern sie sind ähnlich wie diese gezeugt worden und ‹auf die Welt gekommen›.

In dieser spezifischen Qualität von Abgüssen realisierte sich eine Interaktion von Mensch und Natur, ‹ars› und ‹natura›, die in der Konsequenz weit über die bildenden Künste hinausreichte. Das bildgebende Verfahren simulierte Milieu und Prozess einer seltenen Variante natürlicher Zeugung und von dieser symbolischen Anverwandlung ist die Technologie selbst restlos durchdrungen. Die dabei entstehenden Bildwerke waren somit nicht nur der Ausweis eines spezifischen Wissens über Natur, sondern sie waren ein Verfahren – genau dort, wo die Ordnung der belebten Natur *nicht* durch die übliche Abfolge der Generationen gewährleistet wird – technisch in den Prozess der Hervorbringung von Leben einzusteigen. Eine gewisse Unvollkommenheit der Spontanzeugung mag dabei zusätzlich kunsttheoretisch attraktiv gewesen sein. Aristoteles zufolge waren Lebewesen, die auf diese Weise entstehen, vor allem deshalb imperfekt, ja nutzlos, weil bei ihnen die Weitergabe einer ähnlichen, artspezifischen Natur nicht gewährleistet sei.⁴² Wenn es in Abguss und Abformung gelingt, die Gestalt eines vorgängigen Lebewesens auf höchst präzise Weise zu übertragen, dann verändert Kunst somit tatsächlich Natur insofern, als sie die von Natur aus unsteten Eigenschaften bestimmter Lebewesen gleichsam stabilisiert.

In den Abgüssen offenbart sich somit ein Anspruch, der in den Kern der Unterscheidung von ‹ars› und ‹natura› zielt. Vom künstlerischen Prozess her lässt sich sagen: Abgüsse nach der Natur lösen zugleich ein *techne*-Modell plastischer Kunst ein, dass schon Aristoteles selbst in seinen biologischen Schriften verwendete – und sie überbieten dieses Modell.⁴³ Indem die Kunst das Metall dazu bringt, wie von selbst die Gestalt von Tieren und Pflanzen anzunehmen, initiiert sie als seminales Prinzip eine Selbstbewegung des Stoffes und setzt einen Entstehungsprozess in Gang, der eigentlich als eine besondere Potenz *allein* der Natur zukam.⁴⁴ Dabei wird *nicht* versucht, den Kunststatus der Werke zu leugnen. – Vielmehr fingiert die Kunst im Abguss eine Aufhebung jener Differenz von inneren und äußeren bildenden Kräften und Potenzen, die für die Unterscheidung von Natur und Kunst stets konstitutiv war.⁴⁵ Die Verwerfung kategorialer Grenzen ist dabei eine doppelte: Die Kunst gewinnt ein Vermögen, das weit hinausreicht über jene bloß äußeren, an der Oberfläche wirksamen und akzidentiellen Veränderungen natürlicher Dinge, die gemeinhin als der beschränkte Kreis ihrer Wirkungen galt. In die Natur wiederum wird über die Kunst genau in jenem Bereich ein Kontinuität- und Steuerbarkeit versprechendes Prinzip implantiert, wo es ihr selbst abgeht. In diesem doppelten Ineinandergreifen liegt ein Versprechen, das den Wert und Status der bildenden Künste enorm steigert. Sie können nun für sich beanspruchen, nicht mehr – wie seit der Antike – die Natur lediglich in ihren Erscheinungen imitieren zu können, sondern es scheint, als seien sie ihrerseits prinzipiell in der Lage – wie die Medizin oder die Agrikultur – die Natur selbst im Sinne des Menschen zu verbessern.⁴⁶

Teilhabe an den nährenden Kräften der Natur
Mag sein, dass seit Aristoteles die durch Spontanzeugung entstandenen Tiere als niedere Lebewesen galten. Hinzu kamen seit dem Mittelalter vielfältige moralisch negative Konnotationen und Semantiken. Gleichwohl weist der Prozess der Spontanzeugung eine Eigenheit auf, die sich keineswegs dieser naturkundlich-allegorischen Lesart fügt und die ein neues Licht auf die große Verbreitung dieser Kleinplastiken wirft.

Da der Impuls zur Hervorbringung eines neuen Exemplars bei dieser Art der Zeugung allein vom jeweils einzelnen Lebewesen ausgeht, ist für diese Tiere zunächst ein ungewöhnlicher Grad an Autonomie charakteristisch: Gerade jene Funktion, hinsichtlich der alle anderen Lebewesen *per se* als einzelne Individuen nichts zuwege bringen, erfüllt hier jedes Exemplar aus sich selbst. Im weiteren Verlauf jedoch kehren sich diese gegensätzlichen Merkmale um. Aristoteles beschreibt den Prozess des Wachstums in den befruchteten Eiern aller geschlechtlich Zeugenden als einen von der Aussenwelt abgeschlossenen autarken Vorgang, in dem der Körper der heranwachsenden Nachkommen zunächst alles, was er braucht, aus dem Ei bezieht. Deutlich wird diese Entwicklungsphase als Zustand der Isolation bzw. Abkapselung von der umgebenden Natur beschrieben.[47]

Bei der Spontanzeugung hingegen ist dies grundsätzlich anders. Hier wird die Entwicklung einer ‹Larve› als Reifeprozess geschildert, der unter direkter Mitwirkung der Elemente erfolgt und eines aus ihnen sich speisenden ‹pneuma› – Lufthauch, Atem und Lebenswärme.[48] Diese Phase der Spontanzeugung ist somit in besonderer Weise durch ein komplexes Zusammenspiel universeller Substanzen und Kräfte der Natur gekennzeichnet. Die Autonomie der Zeugung ‹aus sich› geht über in einen Prozess der Entfaltung, der unter unmittelbarer Teilhabe an den elementaren Bedingungen und Ressourcen des Lebens vonstatten geht. An Wachstum und Reife einer jeden Larve ist die Natur somit in einem weit umfassenderen Sinne unmittelbar beteiligt, als dies bei der geschlechtlichen Fortpflanzung der Fall ist. – Entscheidend dabei ist, dass diese Orte der Fäulnis und der Zersetzung zugleich als Milieus verstanden werden, in denen nährende Komponenten optimal zusammenwirken.

Diese besondere nutritive Beziehung zur großen Natur, dem Makrokosmos, scheint sich wiederum in markanten Formen der Verwendung von Naturabgüssen und -abformungen zu spiegeln. Zum einen wurden diese Bildwerke häufig in Zusammenhänge eingebunden, die mehr oder weniger unmittelbar mit menschlicher Nahrungsaufnahme verbunden waren. Dies gilt für zahlreiche Lavabo-Garnituren, die zum Waschen der Hände bei Tisch bestimmt waren – auch dann, wenn die Prunkausführungen dieser Becken und Kannen vermutlich nicht wirklich benutzt worden sind. Noch unmittelbarer war die Verbindung mit dem Essen bei Tellern, Krügen und Schalen, die sich zur Präsentation von Früchten anboten; seinen es Keramiken wie jene aus der Palissy-Werkstatt oder der erwähnte *Merkelsche Tafelaufsatz* von Jamnitzer. Pointiert wurde dieser Zusammenhang in so genannten ‹Schauessen›: abgeformten Speisen, die nach ‹niederen Tieren›, wie etwa Fischen hergestellt wurden, oder auch nach Früchten, Bratwürsten und Konfekt.[49] Der gedeckte Tisch und essbare Dinge zeichnen sich so als markante Umgebung von Naturabgüssen ab. Die wahrscheinlich komplexesten Arrangements, in denen zudem die suggestive Lebendigkeit der Abgüsse durch die Gemeinschaft mit tatsächlich lebenden Tieren gesteigert wurde, waren indessen künstliche Grotten.

Joseph Furttenbach, *Architectura privata*..., Augsburg 1641, Tab. 11, Detail.

Neben jenen *rustiques figulines* wie sie Bernard Palissy für seine berühmten Grotten-Projekte vorsah,[50] bevölkerten vielfach auch Abgüsse aus Metall diese kunstvoll arrangierten Orte einer ursprünglich wilden Natur. Dies berichtet etwa der Kunstagent Philipp Hainhofer 1611 von einer Grotte in der neuen Münchner Residenz;[51] besonders aufschlussreich sind hierzu allerdings die Ausführungen des Architekten, Feuerwerkers und Sammlers Joseph Furttenbach. In dessen *Itinerarium Italiae* von 1627 finden sich mehrteilige Kompositionen, in denen farbenprächtige Blumen aus bunten Muscheln auf einer mit Korallenzinken besetzten Gesteinsformation emporwachsen. Der Boden ist bevölkert von Schneckenhäusern sowie von Abgüssen von Eidechsen und Fröschen.[52] Neben dieser ausgiebig beschriebenen skulpturalen Gruppe empfahl Furttenbach an anderer Stelle, ganze Wandpartien mit diesen «Thierlein» auszustaffieren.[53]

In seiner *Architectura privata* von 1641 findet sich der Querschnitt durch das Grottenhäuschen in seinem eigenen Garten in Ulm.[54] Im Zentrum steht hier eine große Brunnenschale; das Becken ist mit Wasser gefüllt und wird von lebenden kleinen Fischen bewohnt. Der Beckengrund ist lückenlos mit Felsgestein und Meergewächsen ausgelegt, auf denen Abgüsse kleiner Krabben sitzen. Auf der Felseninsel in der Mitte ist ein ganzes Ensemble von «in Messing gegossenen Bildlein» angeordnet. Neben Satyrn und einer Nymphe, Vögeln und Affen finden sich Abgüsse von Schildkröten, Schlangen und Krebsen sowie echte Muscheln, Schnecken und Korallenzinken.

Im Zuge seiner Ausführungen gibt der Autor ein *concetto* in Versform für die Ikonografie dieses Brunnens. Analog zu jener Schöpfung, die Gott «ohn Händen hat erbawet», entfaltet es die Betriebsamkeit menschlicher Künste, als Instrumente einer zweiten Schöpfung, deren Schirmherrin Minerva ist. Sie hat sich dabei der feindlichen Mächte von Mars und Vulkan zu erwehren, insbesondere deren kriegerisch entfesselten Gewalten des Feuers. Hierbei hilft ihr nun Neptun, der mit seinen Wassern eine ausgleichende Gegengewalt ins Spiel bringt.[55] Die Tiere, Satyrn und Nymphen auf der Felseninsel sind sowohl bedrohte Schutzbefohlene der Minerva in diesem Konflikt, als auch Bewohner und Repräsentanten einer ‹Urlandschaft›. Sie existiert in der fragilen Balance widerstreitender Naturkräfte und ist dabei zugleich Gründungsmoment und Basis jeder menschlichen Kultur.

Sinnfälliger lassen sich die frappierende Wirkung einzelner Bildwerke sowie deren generative Herkunft aus einem nutritiven Milieu mit der eigenen durch Agrikultur realisierten Nahrungsaufnahme kaum miteinander verbinden. Der Besucher einer solchen Grotte wird Teil eines Biotops, in dem höchste Kunstfertigkeit aus ein und derselben natürlichen Matrix Bilder hervorgehen lässt, die sich von lebenden Wesen kaum unterscheiden lassen, und das zugleich den Menschen als Lebewesen mit Nahrung versorgt.[56]

Diese künstlichen Grotten als Teil von Gartenanlagen waren eine primär höfische Kunstform, die seit etwa Mitte des 16. Jahrhunderts von Italien aus Verbreitung fand. Der im engeren Sinne kunsttheoretische Wert von Abguss und Abformung nach der Natur fand hier einen erweiterten Resonanzraum in der Inszenierung höfischer Bankette. Das Mal sozialer Eliten wurde als Teilhabe an generativen Milieus von einer zugleich archaischen und universellen nutritiven Potenz zelebriert. Die Zerstörung und Substitution von Körpern im Prozedere des Abgießens ist als Paradigma stofflicher Transformationen, zwischen Putrefaktion und erneuter Formgebung, zugleich initiales Moment und symbolische Form dieser nährenden Potenz.[57] Sie manifestiert sich außerdem etwa in den zahlreichen Spielarten bildlicher ‹imitatio› der Speisen selbst, wie sie für die Tischkultur der Renaissance bekannt sind. Die ikonische Belebung der Speisen und Geschirre war dabei eine Variante; eine andere waren die figürlichen Maskierungen von Gerichten, etwa wenn eine Hasenpastete in der Gestalt eines Löwen auftrat.[58] Aus diesem Potential an Transformationen bildet und erhält sich nicht nur das Leben eines jeden individuellen Essers und Betrachters, sondern auch die im Leib des Fürsten verkörperte Herrschaft. Die Inszenierungen des Essens greifen ineinander mit den Ikonografien einer fruchtbaren, weiblichen Natur, deren überbordende Produktivität sich in den Metamorphosen bestimmter Stoffe artikulierte.[59] Und sie berührt sich mit Bildschöpfungen, wie den Kompositköpfen Arcimboldos. Zusammengesetzt etwa aus Früchten, stehen hier die Physiognomien von Potentaten selbst, für die abundante Vielfalt einer fortwährend Nahrung spendenden Natur.[60] Naturabgüsse waren in diesem Zusammenhang nicht weniger als *eine* besondere Art künstlerischer Vermittler im Sinne einer kosmologischen Transzendierung weltlicher Herrschaft.

Verbunden mit diesem Aspekt entfaltete sich an den Abgüssen nach der Natur ein spezifisches *Wissen*, das über die notwendigen Kenntnisse in Metallurgie und Gussverfahren hinausreichte. Die Spezifik dieses Wissens lag vor allem in der einzigartigen Zusammenführung von Naturprozessen und bildnerischer Arbeit; ein pragmatisches Moment steht dabei neben einem bestimmten Strang von naturwissenschaftlicher Forschung. Beide seien in einem Ausblick lediglich angedeutet.

Zum einen kam es in diesen Kunstwerken zu einer ebenso kühnen wie fantastischen Koinzidenz von Lebensprozessen und wirtschaftlichem Reichtum. Wenn diese Bildwerke im Zusammenhang von Banketten und höfischen Inszenierungen eine unerschöpfliche Produktivität von Leben verkörperten, dann fand dieser Aspekt eine direkte Entsprechung in einer ökonomischen Realsymbolik. Insbesondere bei Abgüssen aus Silber oder gar Gold, war das konkrete Bildwerk zugleich eine vorübergehende Gerinnung und ein Reservoir an wertbeständigem Edelmetall. In einem durchaus faktischen Sinne waren Naturabgüsse dann nicht nur lebende Bilder, sondern ein «schaz» und ein nur temporär ikonisch gebundenes Kapital.[61] In diesen Bildwerken kreuzten sich somit die Stoffkreisläufe und Transformationen der lebendigen Natur mit dem materialbasierten Wert des Geldes. Es war kein bloßes *Zeichen* von Reichtum, sondern unmittelbare ökonomische Potenz, eine gewisse Menge an Edelmetall nicht nur überhaupt zu besitzen, sondern aus dem Kreislauf von Geld und Waren abzuzweigen und in dieser Form stillzustellen. – Genau dieser Zusammenhang ist allerdings auch ein Grund, weshalb vermutlich der größte Teil dieser Kunstwerke nicht überlebt hat.

Zum anderen hat diese Bildpraxis einen bis heute kaum erschlossenen Beitrag zu einer der tiefgreifendsten Umwälzung in der Europäischen Wissensgeschichte geleistet. Die bildnerische Adaption biologischer ‹Spontanzeugung› erlaubte es nicht nur, die Abgüsse als lebendige Bildkörper zu verstehen. Diese Bildtechnologie lieferte zudem *ein* heuristisch überaus fruchtbares Modell, mit dem es wenige Jahrzehnte nach Conrad Gesner oder Michele Mercator um 1600 Protagonisten wie Ferrante Imperato und Fabio Colonna gelang, tragfähige Konzepte für eine Deutung der so genannten ‹Figurensteine› als Fossilien im modernen Sinne zu entwickeln.[62] Die Geschichte der Naturwissenschaften hat die Entdeckung einer Naturgeschichte in der Zeit häufig geradezu an die Bedingung geknüpft, dass Natur- und Humangeschichte voneinander entkoppelt wurden. – So war es aber nicht! – Wichtige Impulse für eine durchgreifende Historisierung der Natur kamen aus einem kollektiven Gedankenexperiment, in dem der Abguss, neben anderen Bildtechnologien, eine zentrale Rolle spielte. Die Spur dieser Bildwerke durch die Sammlungen der Frühen Neuzeit lässt erkennen, auf welche Weise künstlerische Praxis und empirische Neugier die Imagination zu einer unumkehrbaren Dynamisierung von Natur angetrieben haben.

Anmerkungen

1 Ich danke Joosje van Bennekom, Konservatorin am Rijksmuseum in Amsterdam, sehr herzlich für die wunderbare Gelegenheit, den *Merkelschen Tafelaufsatz* in ihrem Labor aus der Nähe sehen zu können. Nach umfangreichen Restaurierungen wird er voraussichtlich ab März 2013 erneut im Rahmen der Dauerpräsentation zu sehen sein. Dieses Prunkgefäß von Wenzel Jamnitzer kann als das komplexeste erhaltene Beispiel für die Integration von Naturabgüssen in ein größeres Kunstwerk gelten. Grundlegend zu diesem Werk, vgl. Klaus Pechstein, «Der Merkelsche Tafelaufsatz von Wenzel Jamnitzer» in: *Mitteilungen des Vereins für Geschichte der Stadt Nürnberg*, 1974, Bd. 61, S. 90–121.

2 Ernst Kris, «Der style rustique», in: *Jahrbuch der Kunsthistorischen Sammlungen in Wien*, Wien 1926, S. 137–208; sowie Leo Planscig, *Andrea Riccio*, Wien 1927. Gegen den vermeintlichen Naturalismus wendete sich z. B. Pechstein, etwa in: Klaus Pechstein, «Der Goldschmied Wenzel Jamnitzer», in: *Wenzel Jamnitzer und die Nürnberger Goldschmiedekunst 1500–1700*, hg. v. Gerhard Bott, München 1985, S. 57–70, Ausst.-Kat. Nürnberg, Germanisches Nationalmuseum, 1985.

3 Norberto Gramaccini, «Das genaue Abbild der Natur – Riccios Tiere und die Theorie des Naturabgusses seit Cennino Cennini», in: *Natur und Antike in der Renaissance*, Frankfurt a. M. 1985, S. 189–223, Ausst.-Kat. Frankfurt am Main, Liebighaus, Museum alter Plastik, 1985; Andrea Klier, *Naturabguß und Effigies im 16. Jahrhundert*, Berlin 2004.

4 Vgl. Edgar Lein, «‹Wie man allerhand Insecta, als Spinnen, Fliegen, Käfer, Eydexen, Frösche und auch ander zart Laubwerck scharff abgiessen solle, als wann sie natürlich also gewachsen wären› Die Natur als Modell in Johann Kunckels Beschreibungen des Naturabgusses von Planzen und Tieren», in: *Das Modell in der bildenden Kunst des Mittelalters und der Neuzeit*, hg. v. Peter C. Bol, Petersberg 2006, S. 103–119; Edgar Lein, «Über den Naturabguss von Pflanzen und Tieren», in: *Nürnberger Goldschmiedekunst 1541–1868. Band II: Goldglanz und Silberstrahl*, bearb. v. Karin Tebbe, Nürnberg 2007, S. 205–215.

5 Hanna Rose Shell, «Casting Life, Recasting Experience: Bernard Palissy's Occupation between Maker and Nature», in: *Configurations*, 2004, Bd. 12, S. 1–40; William R. Newman, *Promethean Ambitions. Alchemy and the Quest to Perfect Nature*, Chicago 2004, hier S. 145–163; Patricia Falguières, «Sur le renversement du maniérisme», in: *Ernst Kris. Le style rustique* (übers. ins Franz. von Christophe Jouanlanne), Paris 2005, S. 193–266; sowie kürzlich Pamela H. Smith und Tonny Beentjes, «Nature and Art, Making and Knowing. Reconstructing Sixteenth-Century Life Casting Techniques», in: *Renaissance Quarterly*, 2010, Bd. 63, Nr. 1, S. 128–179. Die Praxis der Abgüsse wird hier als exemplarisch für eine ‹artisanal epistemology› des 16. Jahrhunderts entfaltet, vgl. Pamela H. Smith, *The Body of the Artisan. Art and Experience in the Scientific Revolution*, Chicago 2004.

6 Folgende Ausführungen verstehen sich als eine konkrete Weiterführung des von Bredekamp entwickelten Konzepts des ‹substitutiven Bildakts›. Horst Bredekamp, *Theorie des Bildakts*, Frankfurt a. M. 2010, hier bes. S. 173–191.

7 Der volle Name des Autors ist Johann Kunckel von Löwenstern. *Johann Heinrich Zedlers grosses vollständiges Universal-Lexicon aller Wissenschaften und Künste* (64 + 4 Bde.), Leipzig 1731–1754, Bd. 15, Sp. 2125 und Bd. 18, Sp. 249. Zu Leben und Werk Kunckels vgl. Joachim Telle, «Johann Kunckel von Löwenstern», in: *Literaturlexikon*, hg. v. Walther Killy, Gütersloh/München 1990, S. 89/90; Kühlmann entwickelt ausgehend von Kunckels posthum publiziertem *Collegium Physico-Chymicum Experimentale* (1716) zentrale Probleme im Natur-Kunst-Verhältnis vor allem in der paracelsistischen Tradition. Wilhelm Kühlmann, «Amerkungen zum Verhältnis von Natur und Kunst im Theoriezusammenhang des paracelsistischen Hermetismus», in: *Der Naturbegriff in der Frühen Neuzeit. Semantische Perspektiven zwischen 1500 und 1700*, hg. v. Thomas Leinkauf, Tübingen 2005, S. 87–108, hier S. 87/88.

8 Vgl. Günter Rau, «Das Glas-Laboratorium des Johann Kunckel auf der Pfaueninsel in Berlin. Archäologische Untersuchungen 1973/74», in: *Ausgrabungen in Berlin*, 1974, Bd. 5, S. 155–174.

9 Trotz Erwähnung der *Kunst- und Werckschul* bereits bei Ernst Kris und Arbeiten von Edgar Lein, die sich neben technischen Aspekten vor allem auf Kunckels Modell-Konzept fokussierten, blieben die im Folgenden hervorgehobenen Aspekte dieser Quelle bislang unbeachtet. Vgl. Kris 1926 (wie Anm. 2), S. 143; Lein 2004 (wie Anm. 4); Lein 2007 (wie Anm. 4). Alle Angaben im Folgenden beziehen sich auf folgende drei Publikationen von Kunckel nach dem Exemplaren der Herzog August Bibliothek Wolfenbüttel: Johann Kunckel, *Ars Vitraria experimentalis oder Vollkommene Glasmacher-Kunst ...*, Frankfurt/Leipzig 1679; Johann Kunckel (?), *Der Curieusen Kunst- und Werck-Schul [...] 2 Theil [...] Von einem sonderbaren Liebhaber der Natürlichen Künste und Wissenschaften*, Nürnberg 1696; Johann Kunckel, *Der neu aufgerichteten und vergrösserten in sechs Bücher oder Theilen verfassten curieusen Kunst- und Werck-Schul*, Nürnberg 1707.

10 Kunckel 1696 (wie Anm. 9). Der Abguss wird hier in Teil 1, Kap. 50–54, S. 446–495 behandelt.
11 Die Tötung durch Ertränken wird z. B. empfohlen, wenn man Insekten auf Pflanzen arrangieren will. Ebd., T. 1, S. 463, sowie allgemein für größere Tiere, wobei die drohende Zerstörung von deren Oberfläche zu verhindern sei: «So du also Nattern / Eyderen oder Frösch formen willst / so ertränke sie zuvor in Wein und Essig / der Essig ist ihnen zu starck / frisst ihnen die Haut ab / aber der Wein thut es nicht / und ist besser hierzu /...», ebd., T. 1, S. 464.
12 Ebd., T. 1, S. 447. Beide Bezeichnungen finden sich bereits in den vergleichsweise kurzen Ausführungen zum Abgießen von Pflanzen in der *Ars Vitraria*. Kunckel 1679 (wie Anm. 9), T. 2, S. 73.
13 Ebd., T. 1, S. 447.
14 Mehrfach zu findende Formulierungen lauten etwa: «alsdann brennt man das inwendige Thierlein aus / und lässets glühen ...». Ebd., T. 1, S. 483. Weitere Beispiele hierfür: Ebd., T. 1, S. 450 u. S. 454.
15 Ebd., T. 1, S. 466.
16 Ebd., T. 1, S. 487.
17 Als alternative Verfahren werden dabei nachträglich der Blasebalg und die «Sprütze» als Instrumente für diesen Arbeitsgang erwähnt: «Wann nun solche [die Form, R. F.] erkaltet / so musst du die Asche von dem verbrannten Kraut entweder durch Anziehung des Athems / oder mit einem Blassbalg / durch Aufhebung desselben oberen Theils / heraus ziehen.» Ebd., T. 1, S. 450; sowie: «Wann du die Formen also ausgeglühet hast / und daß sie bald kalt sind / so nimm sie / und schneide den Guß oben fein weit aus / zeuch dann den Aschen mit dem Athem an dich heraus / oder mit einer Sprützen / welche feucht ist / aber doch keine nässen mehr in sich hat ...». Ebd., T. 1, S. 455. Auch dieses Verfahren wurde hinsichtlich der Pflanzen bereits in der *Ars Vitraria* erwähnt. Kunckel 1679 (wie Anm. 9), T. 2, S. 74.
18 Kunckel 1696 (wie Anm. 9), T. 1, S. 483; Auch zur Reinigung der im «Särglein» entstandenen Gussform etwa wird die alternative Verwendung von Quecksilber empfohlen. Ebd., S. 450.
19 Zum Quecksilber und seiner Ikonografie vgl. Allison B. Kavey, «Mercury Falling. Gender Malleability and Sexual Fluidity in Early Modern Popular Alchemy», in: *Chymists and Chymistry. Studies in the History of Alchemy and Early Modern Chemstry*, hg. v. Lawrence M. Principe, Sagamor Beach 2007, S. 125–136.
20 Aristotcles, *Von der Seele*, nach d. Übers. v. Willy Theiler, bearb. v. Horst Seidl (Aristoteles Philosophische Schriften, Bd. 6), Hamburg 1995, I, 3, 406 b, S. 13.
21 Kunckel 1696 (wie Anm. 9), T. 1, S. 482.
22 Ebd., T. 1, S. 485.
23 «E quello che è più, alcune terre e ceneri che a ciò s'adoperano sono venute in tanta finezza che si gettano d'argento e d'oro le ciocche della ruta e ogni altra sottile erba o fiore, agevolmente e tanto bene che cosi belli riescono come il naturale. Nel che si vede questa arte essere in maggior eccellenza che non era al tempo degli antichi.» Giorgio Vasari, *Le vite. De' piu eccellenti pittori, scultori e architettori, nelle redazione de 1550 e 1568* (6 Bde.), hg. u. bearb. v. Rosanna Bettarini u. Paola Barocchi, Florenz 1966–1987, Bd. 1, S. 103.
24 «Sie schmelzen die schönsten Farben von Glas und haben das Silberätzen am höchsten gebracht, was sie aber von Thierlein, Würmlein, Kräutern und Schnecken von Silber giessen, und die silbernen Gefäße damit zieren, dass ist vorhin nicht erhöret worden. Wie sie mich dann mit einer ganzen silbernen Schnecken, von allerlei Blümlein und Kräutlein gegossen, verehret haben, welche Blättlein und Kräutlein also subtil und dünn sind, dass sie auch ein Anblasen wehig macht, aber in dem allen geben sie Gott allein die Ehre.» *Des Johann Neudörfer Schreib und Rechenmeister zu Nürnberg Nachrichten von Künstlern und Werkleuten daselbst. Aus dem Jahre 1547*, hg. v. G. W. K. Lochner, Wien 1875, S. 126.
25 Kunckel 1696 (wie Anm. 9), S. T. 1, S. 482.
26 Ebd., T. 1, S. 463.
27 Ebd., T. 1, S. 465/466.
28 Ebd., T. 1, S. 466.
29 Ebd., T. 1, S. 496.
30 Ebd., T. 1, S. 499–501.
31 Vgl. hierzu insbes. Ebd., T. 1, S. 657–663.
32 Einen Überblick über die Breite dieser Tradition mit Quellen und Vermittlern wie Ovid, Virgil, Aristoteles, Averroes und Paracelsus gibt: Newman 2004 (wie Anm. 5), S. 40–42, 58–61, 166–171 und S. 206–208.
33 Die Frühneuzietlichen Referenzen sind: Della Porta, *Magia naturalis* (1558); auf Aldrovandi, *De Animalibus Insectis* (1618) und auf Kirchers *Mundus subterraneus* (1665). Vgl. Kunckel 1696 (wie Anm. 9), T. 1, S. 662 u. 665–667.
34 Gründzüge werden insbesondere dargelegt in: Aristoteles, *Histoire des Animaux*, übers. und hg. v. Pierre Louis, Paris 1968, IV.1, 539a–539b, S. 2/3 und VI.14, 569a–570a, S. 94–97; sowie in: Aristoteles, *De la génération des animaux*, übers. und hg. v. Pierre Louis, Paris 1961, III, 11, 761b–763b, S. 129–135. Verweise beziehen sich im Folgenden mit den Seitenangaben auf diese fanzösische Ausgabe, soweit nicht lateinische Versionen nach Gaza, Scaliger oder Scotus herangezogen werden, die als konkrete Quellen für die Frühe Neuzeit in Betracht kommen.
35 Eingehend zu den beiden Ausgaben nach Gaza und Scaliger: Stefano Perfetti, *Aristotle's Zoology and its Renaissance Commentators*

33

(1521–1601), Leiden 2000, S. 11–27 u. S. 155–181. Gaza wie auch Scaliger charakterisieren diese Art der Zeugung meist als «sponte». Aristoteles, «De generatione Animalium», übers. ins Lateinische von Theodore Gaza (1476), in: *Aristoteles Latine interpretibus variis*, hg. v. Königlich Preussische Akademie, Berlin 1831, Bd. 3, S. 350–384, III. 11, 761a, S. 371; Aristoteles, *Historia Animalium*, übers. ins Lateinische von Joseph Scaliger, Toulouse 1617, V.1, III, S. 515 u. V.1, VIII, S. 518. Scotus hingegen erwähnt regelmäßig Tiere, die «generantur per se». Aristoteles, «De generatione Animalium», übers. ins Lateinische von Michael Scot, hg. v. Aafke M.I. van der Oppenraaij, Teil 3, Buch XV–XIX von: *De Animalibus*, Leiden/New York/Köln 1992, III. 11, 762a, S. 156 u. 157.

36 Besonders betont werden etwa die generativen Potenzen des Meeres: Ebd., III. 11, 761b, S. 129; zum Körper anderer Lebewesen als Zeugungsort: Aristoteles Histoire (wie Anm. 34), V. 31, 556b–557b, S. 56–59.

37 Vgl. Shell 2004 (wie Anm. 5), hier S. 10/11 u. 15–17.

38 Pamela Smith betont diese symbolische Ebene, auf der der ästhetische Naturalismus der Abgüsse als Ausweis des Wissens der Goldschmiede um natürliche Prozesse und alchimistische Verfahren zu verstehen sei. Wie genau beide Momente ineinander greifen, erfährt man allerdings nicht. Vgl. Smith 2004 (wie Anm. 5), S. 119ff; sowie Smith/Beentjes 2010 (wie Anm. 5), hier bes. S. 141–143.

39 Walter Herrmann Ryff, *Der furnembsten, notwendigsten, der gantzen Architectur angehörigen Mathematischen und Mechanischen künst, eygentlicher bericht*, Nürnberg 1547, S. XLIII r.

40 Ebd., S. XLIv. Unter dem starken Akzent den Ryff bekanntlich auf die mathematischen Grundlagen bildender Kunst setzte, spielten Praktiken und die Abgüsse eine ambivalente Rolle. Das Hauptaugenmerk seiner Ausführungen zur Skulptur lag auf dem Menschen und seinen Proportionen – umso bemerkenswerter, sind die ausführlichen Schilderungen von Guspraktiken und die skizzierte Rolle von Naturabgüssen in diesem Zusammenhang.

41 Hier wird von Lysistratos aus Sikyon berichtet, der als erster menschliche Gesichter und Körper mit dem Effekt abgegossen habe. Cajus Plinius Secundus, *Naturalis historiae/Naturkunde*, Bd. XXXV, hg. v. Roderich König u. Gerhard Winkler, Düsseldorf u. Zürich 1997, S. 116/117.

42 Aristoteles Histoire (wie Anm. 34), V. 1, 539b, S. 3. Vgl. auch Aristoteles/Gaza Generatione (wie Anm. 35), I. 18, 723b, S. 354. In Scaligers Übersetzung der *Historia de Animalibus* V. 1 werden die spontan gezeugten Lebewesen in diesem Zusammenhang ausdrücklich als unvollkommen bzw. nutzlos bezeichnet. Aristoteles/ Scaliger Historia (wie Anm. 35), V. 1, VII, S. 518.

43 «Wie nämlich diejenigen, die aus Ton oder irgendeiner anderen feuchten Verbindung ein Lebewesen bilden, irgendeinen festen Körper als Gerüst einziehen und dann darum herum modellieren, in derselben Weise hat die Natur aus dem Fleisch das Lebewesen gebildet.» Aristoteles, *Über die Teile der Lebewesen*, übers. u. erl. v. Wolfgang Kullmann (Aristoteles Werke in deutscher Übersetzung, Bd. 17, Zoologische Schriften Teil I), Berlin 2007, II. 9, 654b, S. 48.

44 In den Ausführungen zur Spontanzeugung wurde diese Formbildung ‹aus sich› verschiedentlich beschrieben. An anderer Stelle setzt Aristoteles explizit die Arbeit eines Künstlers mit der formschaffenden Wirkung des Samens gleich und stellt dieses Prinzip einem so genannten «Entstehen von ungefähr» gegenüber, bei dem der Stoff aus sich selbst bewegt wird. Vgl. Ottfried Höffe (Hg.), *Aristoteles: Die Hauptwerke. Ein Lesebuch*, Tübingen 2009, S. 176/177.

45 Vgl. zu dieser prinzipiellen Unterscheidung: Aristoteles, *Physik*, nach d. Übers. v. Willy Theiler, bearb. v. Horst Seidl (Aristoteles Philosophische Schriften, Bd. 6), Hamburg 1995, II. 2, 192b, S. 25.

46 Vgl. Newman 2004 (wie Anm. 5), S. 69–72.

47 Zur Spezifik der Zeugung im Ei im Unterschied zur Spontanzeugung, vgl. insbes: Aristoteles Génération (wie Anm. 34), III. 11, 762b–763a, S. 132–133.

48 So weist etwa Pierre Luis darauf hin, dass Aristoteles hier von «pneuma» spricht, was in Übersetzungen oft nicht mehr kenntlich aber insofern bedeutsam ist, weil es häufig auch den Atem, Hauch die Lebenssubstanz schlechthin bezeichnet. Ebd., III. 11, 761b, S. 129. In diesem Sinne hat Gaza den Lufthauch mit «spiritus» übersetzt und in die belebende Wirkung eines «calor animalis» überführt. Aristoteles/Gaza Generatione (wie Anm. 35), III. 11, 762a/b, S. 372. In äußerst kompakter Form findet sich dieses Zusammenwirken der vier Elemente und ihrer Qualitäten bereits bei Scotus: «Animalia ergo in terra et humido, quoniam in terra est pars aquae et in aqua est pars aeri, et in eis est calor animae. Et ita sund arbores in terra et in aqua, et aliquo modo dicimus qoud omnes istae res sunt plenae virtute animae.» Aristoteles/Scotus Generatione (wie Anm. 35), III. 11, 762a, S. 157.

49 Vgl. Johann Baptist Fickler, *Das Inventar der Münchner herzoglichen Kunstkammer von 1598*, hg. v. Peter Diemer, München 2004, S. 129/130, Nr. 1456 (1348)–1458 (1350); Dorothea Diemer u.a. (Hg.), *Die Münchner Kunstkammer*, München 2008, Bd. 1, T. 1, S. 468/469, Nr. 1456 (1348)–1458 (1350).

50 Vgl. Bernard Palissy, *Recepte véritable par laquelle tous les hommes de la France pourront apprendre à multiplier et augmenter leurs tresors ...* (La Rochelle 1563), bearb. u. hg. v. Frank Lestringant, Paris 1996, S. 51–242, hier S. 142/143. Seit der ‹Wiederentdeckung› von Abgüssen und ‹style rustique› durch Ernst Kris wurde immer wieder auf diese Kombination hingewiesen: vgl. Philippe Morel, *Les Grottes maniéristes en Italie au XVIe siècle. Théâtre et alchimie de la nature*, Paris 1998; speziell in Hinblick auf Palissy in dieser Tradition: Anne-Marie Lecoq, «The Garden of Wisdom of Bernard Palissy», in: *The History of Garden Design. The Western Tradition from the Renaissance to the Present Day*, London 1991, S. 69–80.

51 «Die Grotta, so in disem newen baw, ist von rechtem felsen zusammen gemacht, ist von eingehauenen Zellen, mit Dannen vnd wilden bäumen besetzet, quilt ein wässerlin auss dem felsen herauss, dass macht ein bächlein vnd weyerlin» – mit lebenden Forellen und – «Imm bächlein wie das wasser heraussquillet, ligen in bley gegossene Schlangen, Edexen, Krotten, Krebs ...». Philipp Hainhofer, «Die Reisen des Augsburgers Philipp Hainhofer nach Eichstädt, München und Regensburg in den Jahren 1611, 1612 und 1613», hg. v. Christian Häutle, in: *Zeitschrift des Historischen Vereins für Schwaben und Neuburg*, 1881 (8. Jg,), S. 64.

52 Joseph Furttenbach, *Newes Itinerarium Italiae...*, Ulm 1627, S. 221/222 und Tab. 18. Als 1663 mit den *Feriae Architectonicae* posthum kleinere Abhandlungen vor allem zur Baukunst und Artillerie von Furttenbach erschienen, wurden hierin erneut auch die „kleinen Thierlein" aufgegriffen, mit denen künstliche Grotten auszustatten seien. Joseph Furttenbach, *Feriae Architectonicae ...* , o.O. 1663, T. 7, S. 88/89.

53 So etwa in der *Architectura civilis* von 1628, wo zur Einrichtung einer Grotte in einem Palazzo empfohlen wird, es sollten: «... auch mit mancherley kriechenden Thierlein die Wänd also erfüllt und gestaffiert werden / dass man ein geraume Zeit / biß alles *curios* beschauwet / mit Lust zubringen wirdt.» Joseph Furttenbach, *Architectura civilis. Das ist Eigentliche Beschreibung wie man nach bester Form und gerechter Regul Fürs erste Palläst / mit dero Lust: und Thiergarten / darbey auch Grotten [...] aufführen unnd erbawen soll*, Ulm 1628, S. 42.

54 In der eingehenden Beschreibung seines eigenen Hauses bildet die Grotte – neben der Kunstkammer – einen deutlich akzentuierten Schwerpunkt. Joseph Furttenbach, *Architectura privata ...*, Augsburg 1641, S. 19–58.

55 Ebd., S. 63–65.

56 Vgl. auch hierzu Palissy, für den eine Ökonomie dieser Natur tatsächlich der übergeordnete sowohl naturphilosophische wie politisch relevante Horizont seiner Kunst war. Vgl. Danièle Duport, *Le jardin et la nature. Ordre et variété dans la litterature de la Renaissance*, Genf 2002, S. 63–67.

57 Zu dieser zwangsläufig zerstörerischen und Form erhaltenden Dimension des Essens und ihrer religiös-symbolischen Bearbeitung: vgl. Hartmut Böhme, «Transsubstantiation und symbolisches Mahl. Die Mysterien des Essens und die Naturphilosophie», in: *Zum Naturbegriff der Gegenwart*, Bd. 1, Stuttgart 1994, S. 139–158.

58 Vgl. François Quiviger, *The sensory World of Italian Renaissance Art*, Princeton 2010, S. 158–155.

59 Vgl. Rebecca Zorach, *Blood, Milk, Ink, Gold: Abundance and Excess in the French Renaissance*, Chicago 2005.

60 Vgl. *Arcimboldo. 1526–1593*, hg. v. Silvia Verino-Pagden, Milano 2008, insbes. S. 124–148, Ausst.-Kat. Wien, Kunsthistorisches Museum, 2008; Thomas DaCosta Kaufmann, *Arcimboldo. Visual Jokes, Naural History and Still Life Painting*, Chicago 2010, insbes. S. 50–68.

61 So berichtet der erwähnte Hainhofer einem fürstlichen Auftraggeber: «... der Lencker hat noch ain ganz silberne grosse schlangen, und etlich klain edexen, so der alt Lorenz auf der walck gegossen, hat Ihme für ain edex fl. 8 geben, er will aber nichts darvon verkauffen, sondern helts für ain schaz auf». Philipp Hainhofer, «Des Augsburger Patriciers Philipp Hainhofer Beziehungen zum Herzog Philipp II. von Pommern Stettin. Correspondenzen aus den Jahren 1610–1619», hg. v. Oscar Doering, in: *Quellenschriften für Kunstgeschichte und Kunsttechnik des Mittelalters und der Neuzeit* N.F. Bd. 5, Wien 1894/96, S. 79.

62 Eingehend zu diesem Prozess vgl. Robert Felfe, *Naturform und beildenrischer Prozess. Elemente einer Wissensgeschichte in der Kunst des 16. und 17. Jahrhunderts* (Habilitation 2011), Drucklegung in Vorbereitung.

Nikola Irmer
Promethean Boldness

For Charles Waterton ‹Promethean boldness› was a scientific as well as an artistic virtue. His *Wanderings in South America*, 1825, «contained instructions on how to become ‹in ornithology, what Michel Angelo was in sculpture. In order to attain a Michelangelesque fusion of anatomical accuracy and classic beauty, the taxidermist must ‹pay close attention to the form and attitude of the bird … the proportion each curve, … or expansion of any particular part bears to the rest of the body … you must possess Promethean boldness, and bring down fire, and animation as it were, into your preserved specimen.› This act of revivification paradoxically involved discarding the bird's perishable body, retaining only the skin and a few bones.»[1]

The taxidermist's art is a key technique of the Natural History collection. The specimens are very artificial constructs. In order to make one bird it is often necessary to use the feathers and body parts of several different birds. So even if they look startlingly ‹natural› they are highly sophisticated artefacts. The storeroom of the Natural History Museum Berlin houses an amazing collection of birds, witness to the collection mania of the 19th century. To be confronted with this plethora of specimens—dead animals, eerily lifelike—is quite an unsettling experience.

In the pursuit of knowledge, scientists in the 19th century were driven to amass specimens in a search for new species and for new ways of classifying them. So a vast number of animals were hunted, killed, shipped to Europe, prepared as specimens and assembled in the collections. The animals' individual bodies were of interest primarily as representatives of their species. The process of preparation (‹stuffing› or ‹pickling›) turned the animal into a specimen and as such it carried meaning only in the context of a sequence or a system of taxonomy, homology etc.

Man's relationship to animals manifests itself in these collections as dominated by an attempt at controlling and taming the abundance of nature by systems of classification, ordering and collecting.

But the viewer today can have quite a different experience when seeing the exhibits. This is what the paintings and drawings try to show. Fully aware of the intended meanings and history of the collections, the paintings are yet an attempt to tell a different story: that looking at the specimens in the storeroom can be an uncanny encounter. When lit up, the birds' bodies come to life and it is possible to look at them as the remains of something that was once alive, that had a life history and character. In the medium of painting I am mediating this divide by the fact that I am looking at something highly artificially constructed, which exerts a strange fascination and invites my engagement. The irony here is of course heightened by the fact that a painter could never dream of painting something as elusive as birds unless they were dead.

The paintings and drawings pursue a poetic potential of natural history that is inherent in the practice of collecting and scientific research—the accompanying desire to revivify the mass of dead animals which were categorized and to create a self-delusional communion with the animals.

Annotation

1   Diana Donald, *Picturing Animals in Britain*, New Haven u. London, 2007, p. 59.

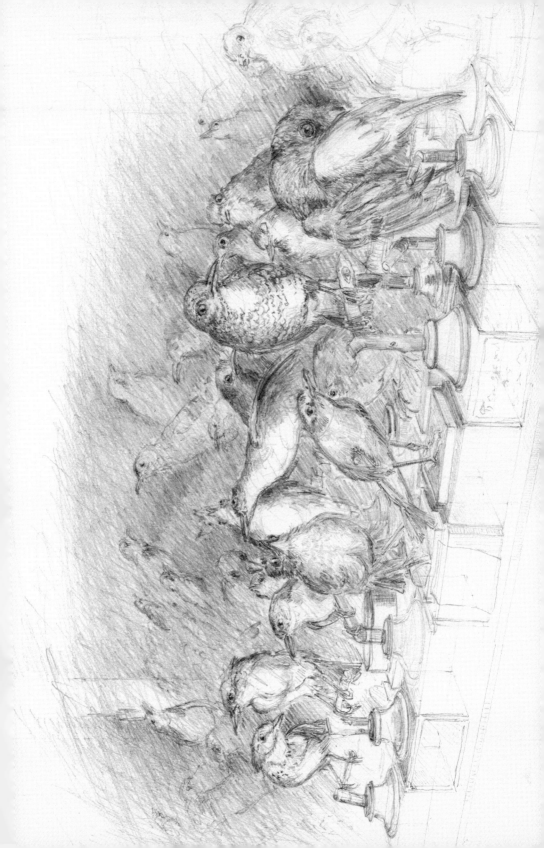

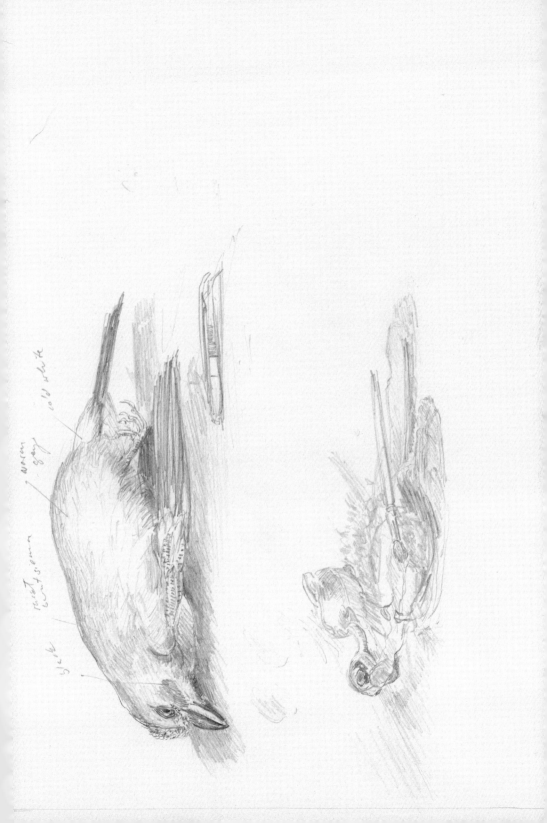

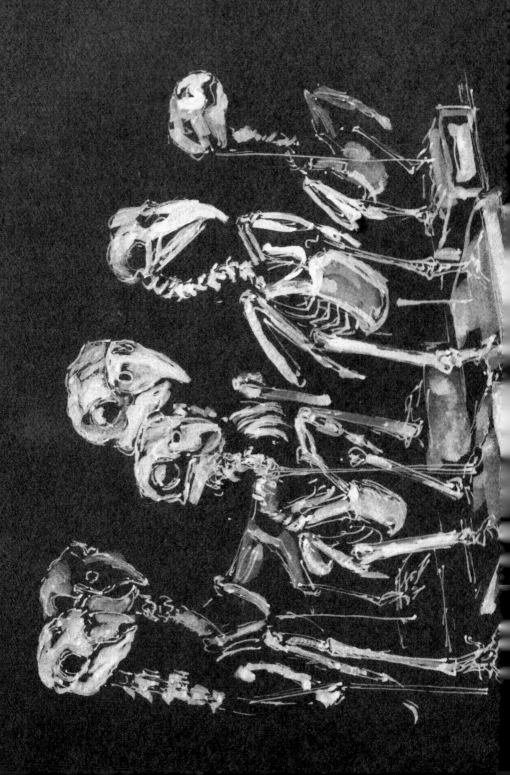

Cioran
sur l'éducation
du crocodile

Golden + tufted
Lion Tamarin
– east coast of
Brazil

Emperor
Tamarin
West Brazil, east Peru

The Force of the Mother's Imagination upon her Foetus in Utero – Daniel Turner 1667–1741
1730

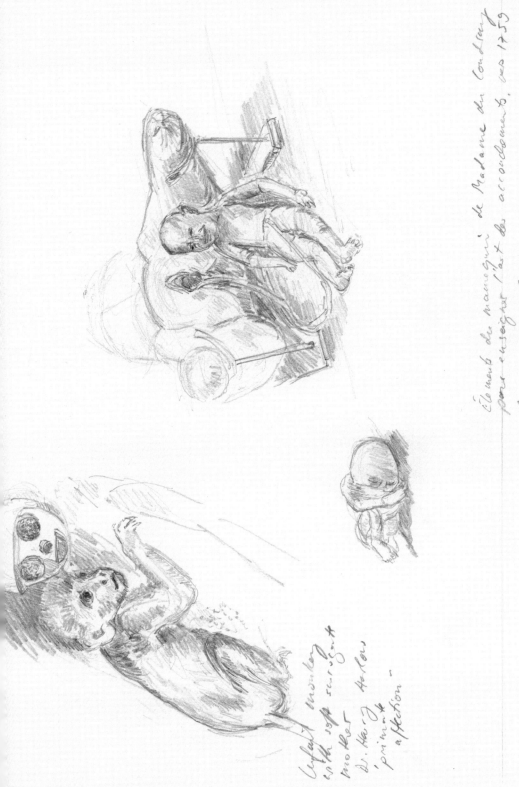

Enfant montrant
intérêt sur-sur-sent
mother
W. Harry Harlow
"primate
affection"

Éléments du mannequin de Madame du Coudray
pour enseigner l'art des accouchements, vers 1759
Rouen musée Flaubert d'histoire de la médecine

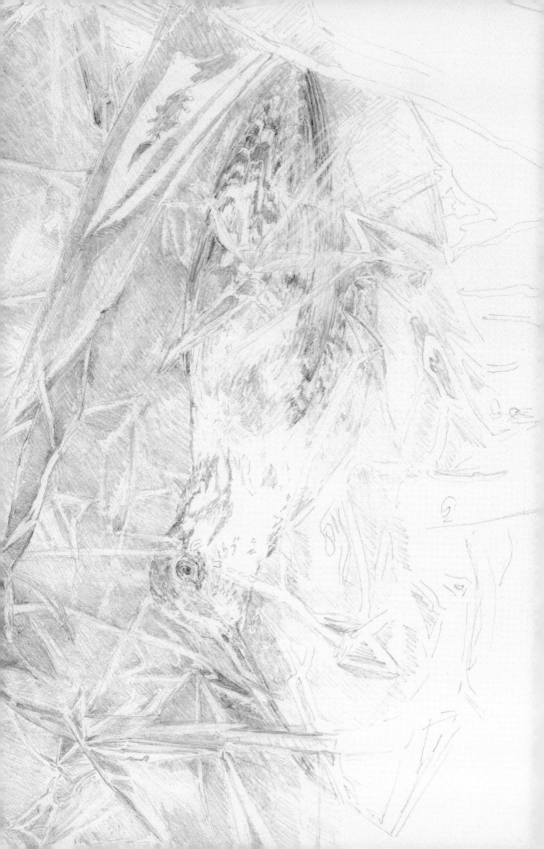

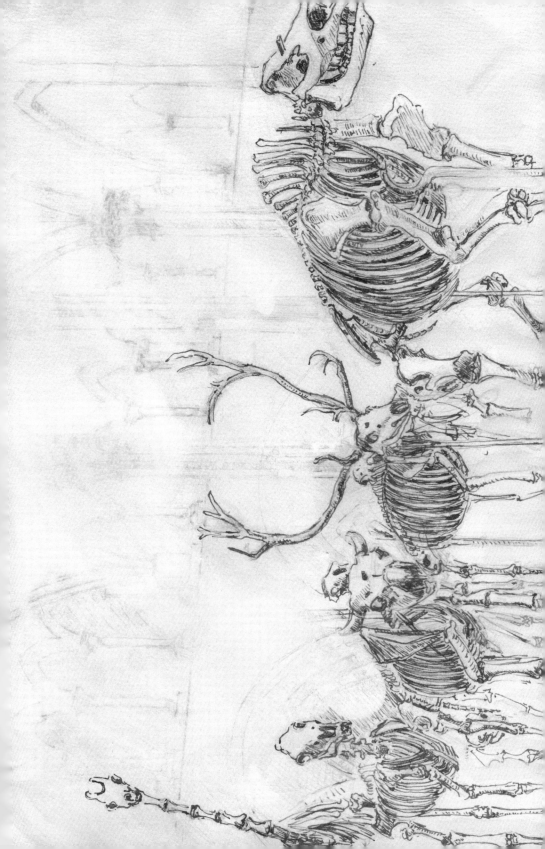

Henrike Haug
«Wunderbarliche Gewechse».
Bergbau und Goldschmiedekunst im 16. Jahrhundert

Gabriel Kaldemarck formuliert 1587 in seiner Schrift *Bedenken wie eine Kunst-Cammer aufzurichten seyn möchte*:

> In einer wohlbestelten KunstCammer sollen fürnehmlich dreierlei sachen zu finden sein. Erstlich runde Bilder. Zum andern Gemele, und zum dritten wunderbarliche In- und auslendische Gewechse. von Metallen, Stein, Holcz, Kreutern, so uff der Erden, in der Erden, in Wasser und Meer gefunden wirdt...[1]

Zu der genannten dritten Kategorie zählen besonders schöne Erzfunde, deren Form, Kontext und Aufgabe in diesem Artikel untersucht werden soll. Diese Erzstufen wurden als *Handsteine* von den Bergleuten aus dem normalen Verhüttungsprozess ausgesondert und waren begehrte und sehr teure Sammlerstücke, die entweder in natürlicher Form, leicht gefasst auf einem Sockel oder künstlerisch überformt in den Kunstkammern präsentiert wurden.[2]

Ihr Name (*lapides manuales*) stammt von der Größe dieser natürlichen Funde und übertrug sich von dort auf die überformten Stücke, in die Goldschmiede narrative Szenen einarbeiteten.[3] Ein besonders eindrucksvolles Beispiel ist der Handstein von Caspar Ulich, bei dem der Künstler in eine reine Silbererzstufe die Auferstehung Christi auf der Vorderseite und die Begegnung zwischen Kaiser Karl V. und dem französischen König Franz I. nach der Schlacht von Pavia (1525) auf der Rückseite geschnitten hat.[4] (Abb. 1). Heute stehen diese Stücke meist isoliert in (Kunstgewerbe-)Museen und haben ihre einstige Bedeutung und Rolle im wissenschaftlichen, wirtschaftlichen und damit auch politischen Umfeld ihrer Entstehungszeit verloren. Dieser Artikel will den Kontext, in dem sie betrachtet, gesammelt und inszeniert wurden, rekonstruieren und dabei einige der Akteure vorstellen, die sie auffanden, sie schufen und in deren wissenschaftliche wie politisch-wirtschaftliche Diskurse sie integriert waren. Nur so werden sie erneut als signifikante Schauobjekte präsent, die im 16. Jahrhundert im Mittelpunkt nicht allein ästhetischer, sondern auch naturwissenschaftlicher Diskussionen standen.

Die größte Sammlung von durch Goldschmiede überarbeiteten Handsteinen – 32 an der Zahl – wird heute im Kunsthistorischen Museum in Wien verwahrt. Alle diese Objekte entstammen der Kunstkammer von Erzherzog Ferdinand II. von Tirol in Schloss Ambras.[5] Das Nachlassinventar dieser Sammlung von 1596 nennt dort 41 Handsteine im dritten der große Schauschränke in der Mitte des Raumes, darüber hinaus wird in der «Biblioteca oder püecherkunstcamer» ein Tisch beschrieben, in dessen Laden sich mehr als 1800 Metalle und Mineralien, Edelsteine und Halbedelsteine, aber auch Fossilien, Korallen, Perlmutt sowie eine große Anzahl von Handsteinen befanden.[6] Das besondere Interesse von Ferdinand II. von Tirol an diesen sonderbar geformten Erzfunden wird aber nicht allein durch die große Anzahl der Objekte in seiner Sammlung bezeugt, sondern spiegelt sich

1   Caspar Ulich, Handstein mit der Darstellung der Auferstehung Christi und der Begegnung zwischen Kaiser Karl V. und dem französischen König Franz I. nach der Schlacht von Pavia, 1525, Kunsthistorisches Museum Wien, Inv. Nr. 4148.

auch in einem Brief, den er im Jahr 1574 an einen böhmischen Bergrichter sandte und in dem er bat, dass man ihm schicke,

> was ihr von ebenmäßigen schönen zierlichen handsteinen, es sei von gediegenem silber, rotguldenerz, auch von allerlei farben, schön wunderbarlichen artigen gezierten gewäxen und gebirgen und was sonst disfalls von seltsamen handsteinen bei diesem bergwerk gebrochen wird, dieweil wir zu solchen und dergleichen handsteinen eine sonder lust und begierd haben.[7]

Diese *sonder Lust und begierd* des Fürsten an den Handsteinen aus dem böhmischen Erzgebirge mag ästhetisch durch die sonderbaren Formen, die erstaunlichen Farben sowie den reinen Materialwert der Objekte begründbar sein, ebenso bedeutend aber waren die wirtschaftlich-politischen Aspekte dieser Sammlertätigkeit: Hielt Ferdinand doch als Statthalter in Böhmen das Bergregal und hatte damit sowohl das Anrecht an und die Zugriffsmöglichkeit auf die dort geförderten Rohstoffe, ein Anrecht, dass durch die Präsentation der Erze in den fürstlichen Sammlungen sichtbaren Ausdruck fand.[8]

Denn das Vorkommen von mineralischen Bodenschätzen im Land und das Auftauchen von Erzstufen in der Kunstkammer hängen ursächlich zusammen; bedeutende Handsteinsammlungen finden sich nur im Umkreis jener Fürsten, deren Territorien Anteile am Erzgebirge aufwiesen, also Böhmen und Sachsen.[9] So präsentierten die sächsischen Kurfürsten in der 1560 gegründeten Kunstkammer in Dresden in der sechsten Kammer – «Sachen von Natur rar und künstlich» – mehrere besonders große und schöne Erzstufen und Handsteine:

> Weiter werden in einem Aufziehe-Schrancke und in einem andern Repositorio hochschätzbare Metalla gesehen / als pur gewachsen Silber aus hiesigen Land-Bergwercken / Gold / Zien und anders / wie ingleichen mitten in dieser Kammer vier grosse hohe Stuffen / so aus hiesigen Land-Ertz zusammen gesetzt.[10]

Die Handstein-Bestände der fürstlichen Sammlungen in Dresden und Schloss Ambras spiegeln damit anschaulich die Bedeutung des Erzgebirges als Zentrum des europäischen Bergbaus des 16. Jahrhunderts wider.[11]

Dieses Mittelgebirge bildet die natürliche Grenze zwischen Sachsen und Böhmen. Kurfürst August hatte seinerseits als Landesherr von Sachsen das hiesige Bergregal inne und damit direkten Zugriff auf die gefundenen Bodenschätze, analog zu Erzherzog Ferdinand II. von Tirol, der seit 1547 als Verwalter seines Vaters Kaiser Ferdinand I. in Böhmen (im Amt eines Vizekönigs) tätig war und dort, auf Wunsch seines Bruders, Kaiser Maximilian II., bis 1567 das Amt des böhmischen Statthalters ausübte.

Vor diesem Hintergrund waren die Handsteine durch das Material an jene Regionen gebunden, in denen diese Gewächse der Erde gefunden wurden. Darüber hinaus aber waren sie translozierbar und wurden durch das Entnehmen aus dem Bergwerk und das Übertragen in eine Sammlung ausstellbare Zeichen, die auf den ehemaligen Fundort sowie die reichen Bodenschätze des Landes und dessen blühende Montanindustrie verweisen.

St. Joachimsthal – ein Zentrum des Montanwesens und seine Akteure
Einer der bedeutendsten Orte sowohl des Silberbergbaus als auch der frühen Metallurgie ist ohne Zweifel St. Joachimsthal (Jachymov), eine alte Bergstadt im böhmischen Teil des Erzgebirges. 1470 waren ergiebige Silbererzvorkommen in Schneeberg und 1492 am Schreckenberg im heutigen Annaberg-Buchholz ent-

deckt worden.¹² Dies löste einen starken Zuzug von Menschen in die Region und die Konzentration von Bergbau aus und führte in kürzester Zeit zur Gründung der heute noch namenhaften Bergstädte Annaberg, Schneeberg, Marienberg und eben auch St. Joachimsthal.

Da der Zugriff auf die vorhandenen Rohstoffe den Reichtum des Landes stärkt und damit dessen politische Handlungsfähigkeit maßgeblich definiert, gehörte es zu den wichtigsten Interessen des Landesherrn, die Bergbau-Industrie zu fördern, die Produktionsbedingungen zu verbessern und die Forschung in diesem Felde zu konzentrieren.[13] Die Zentren der Montanindustrie mit ihren Bergwerken und den das Erz weiterverarbeitenden Betrieben waren dabei zugleich Austauschplätze, in denen unterschiedliche Fachleute aus ihrer Praxis heraus zur Verbesserung des Wissens um Metalle und Mineralien wie auch zur Professionalisierung der Abbaumethoden der Erze beitrugen.

Einer der wichtigsten Protagonisten der frühen Metallurgie ist Georg Agricola.[14] Bekannt sind seine Abhandlungen, so der noch in seiner Zeit als Stadtarzt von St. Joachimsthal 1530 in Basel veröffentlichte *Bermannus, sive de re metallica*, ebenso wie die nachfolgenden Publikationen *De ortu et causis subterraneorum libri V* (1544), *De natura eorum, quae effluunt ex terra libri IV* (1546), *De natura fossilium libri X*, *De veteribus et novis metallis libri II* (beide 1546) und sein Hauptwerk *De re metallica libri XII*, also die zwölf Bücher über den Bergbau, das Hüttenwesen und über die Metalle, das posthum 1556 in Basel bei Hieronymus Froben erschien.[15]

Georg Agricola schuf seine Schriften basierend auf dem Erfahrungsschatz von St. Joachimsthaler Praktikern und durch den Austausch mit ihnen, wie er in seiner ersten montanistischen Schrift protokolliert: Der Bermannus ist in der Form eines lehrhaften Dialoges verfasst, Gesprächspartner sind der Hüttenschreiber von St. Joachimsthal, Lorenz Bermann, von dem Agricola tatsächlich Grundlegendes über Bergbau und Hüttenwesen lernte.[16] Bermann trifft auf dem Marktplatz zwei an naturwissenschaftlichen Fragen interessierte Ärzte; die drei beginnen ein Gespräch und handeln darin alle die Montanindustrie betreffenden Themen ab. Der Gesprächsverlauf kann paradigmatisch für die Neuorientierung der Naturforschung im 16. Jahrhundert stehen, die sich von der Kenntnis und Rezeption der tradierten Autoritäten emanzipiert und dabei immer mehr auf die eigene Erfahrung stützt, diese Erfahrung durch Sammlung, Ordnung und Kategorisierung ausbaut und durch materialbasierte Experimente versucht, bestimmte Gesetzmäßigkeiten zu definieren.

Einer der Ärzte – Johannes Naevius (Johannes Neffe, Stadtarzt in Annaberg) – nimmt während des Dialogs Minerale in die Hand und bemerkt:

> Diese Dinge will ich mir nämlich zu Hause und in aller Ruhe noch sorgfältiger in Augenschein nehmen. So habe ich mir auch einst in Italien häufig Kräuter, häufig auch Fische nach Hause gebracht. Denn so wie in diesem Tal Bermann mit höchster Sorgfalt Bergbaufragen untersucht, hat in Padua Dominico Zeno die Pflanzenwelt und in Venedig Francesco Massaro die Fischwelt studiert.[17]

Hervorzuheben ist die methodische Klammer, die die beiden mit naturwissenschaftlichen Fragen befassten Ärzte und den vor Ort forschenden Praktiker umfasst: sie sind an Materialfragen arbeitende Sammler, die Gesteinsproben mit nach Hause nehmen, um sie dort genauer zu erforschen. Die drei sehen sich dabei selbstverständlich als Teil eines naturwissenschaftlichen Gelehrtennetzwerkes, das St. Joachimsthal und die dort betriebene Mineralogie ideell mit zwei italienischen Forschern verbindet, die im Bereich der Botanik und der Ichthyologie das Wissen erweitern.[18]

Innerhalb des Gelehrtenkreises in St. Joachimsthal und um Agricola ist der Pfarrer der Stadt, Johannes Mathesius, der Mineralien sammelte, als Historiograph der Bergstadt tätig war und 1562 seine berühmten Bergpredigten *Sarepta oder Bergpostille* veröffentliche, von höchster Bedeutung.[19] In seinen Texten offenbart sich Mathesius als profunder Kenner des Bergbaus, der humanistische Gelehrsamkeit mit genauster Kenntnis der montanistischen Praxis verbindet.[20] Darüber hinaus verwob er eindrücklich metallurgische Kenntnisse mit theologischer Spekulation über Art und Natur der Mineralien und ist somit eine erstrangige Quelle zu Fragen der Materialbewertung im 16. Jahrhundert. Als Theologe und Forscher sah er seine Tätigkeit aus zwei Quellen gespeist, aus «Gottes Wort und augenscheinlicher Erfahrung», denn «Erfahrung ist alles, und wer wider die Erfahrung redet oder disputieret, der ist nicht wol bey sich selber.»[21] Dass die Hinwendung zur Materie dabei auch Suche nach Gott ist – das *Buch der Natur* somit als zweite Offenbarung gelesen und gedeutet werden kann – spielt bei Mathesius wie bei vielen Forschern seiner Generation eine wichtige Rolle, sind ihm zufolge doch die Erzvorkommen durch das «Sprechen Gottes in die Erde» entstanden.[22] Seine sechste Predigt ist dem Silber gewidmet, über das er in

> bergleufftiger Weise [reden will], wann es den Namen hat, wo seiner in der Schrift am ersten gedacht wird, wie mancherlei es sei, wo es breche, wie mans gewinn und reine und fein mache und was uns Gott in diese silberne Postill fürgeschrieben oder uns durch das Silber neben seinem Wort erinnern und fürbilden lasse.[23]

Die Predigt liest sich tatsächlich über viele Strecken wie eine Anleitung zum Bergbau, gewinnt aber zusätzliche Bedeutung nicht allein durch die Nennung aller relevanten Bibelstellen, sondern vor allem durch die Deutung des Silbers als Manifest gewordenes Worte Gottes, das ebenso wie ein Text gelesen und erkannt werden will. In dieser Predigt nennt er den schon genannten Handstein von Caspar Ulich:

> Die schöneste stuffe, die ich mein tag gesehen, war ein glaß ertz von etlichen Marcken, darein man die aufferstehung des Sons Gottes mit seinem grab und Wechtern künstlich geschnitten hatte. Da gabs das gewechse, das der leib des Herren eben in weyß silber kam, wechter und grab war schwartz wie bley.[24]

Materialkenntnis, künstlerische Überarbeitung, Integration der biblischen Historie in den Diskurs und darüber hinaus die Betonung des Verweischarakters in Erz und Werk, da der Körper des Auferstehenden in leuchtendem Silber sich von der Dunkelheit des Grabes und der Wächter absetzt, treffen in der Predigt wie im Artefakt zusammen.

Als dritter Forscher neben dem Arzt Agricola und dem Prediger Mathesius ist Johannes Kentmann zu nennen, der exemplarisch für den frühneuzeitlichen *Sammler* steht.[25] War es doch vor allem die Methode des Sammelns und Ordnens, die die Kenntnis der Minerale in der 2. Hälfte des 16. Jahrhunderts stark vermehrte und damit den Grundstein für eine Vertiefung des mineralogischen Wissens überhaupt erst legte.[26] Kentmanns Sammlung ist heute – wie so viele Gelehrtensammlungen des 16. Jahrhunderts – nicht mehr erhalten. Glücklicherweise aber wurde der dazu erstellte Mineralienkatalog mit über 1600 Exponaten durch Conrad Gesner in seiner Kompilation *De Omni Rerum Fossilium Genere, Gemmis, Lapidi-*

bus, Metallis veröffentlicht.²⁷ Kentmanns Text ist die erste erhaltene vollständige Darstellung einer Mineral- und Gesteinssammlung, mit Angabe der genauen Fundorte und unter Anführung der deutschen Vulgärnamen neben den lateinischen; seine Proben stammen größtenteils aus Sachsen. Beispielsweise finden sich im Kapitel der Silberfunde unter der Nr. 13 ein besonderes Stück aus St. Joachimsthal, bei dem Silber mit Tannenholz verwachsen ist, gefolgt von der Nr. 14, einem Handstein aus Annaberg mit unterschiedlichen silberhaltigen Erzen.²⁸

Im Hinblick auf die Sammlertätigkeit als Teilgebiet frühneuzeitlicher Naturforschung ist hervorzuheben, dass Kentmann sich zwar an dem durch Agricola vorformulierten Ordnungssystem orientierte, dieses aber auch variierte: So bespricht beispielsweise Agricola in Buch Acht seiner Re metallica die 8 damals bekannten Metalle: Gold, Silber, Quecksilber, Kupfer, Blei, Zinn, Wismut und Eisen. Dabei kam es ihm vor allem darauf mit an, die Selbständigkeit dieser Metalle zu behaupten, sein Erkenntnisziel aber zwang ihn, mit starken Kategorisierungen zu arbeiten. Anders der Sammler Kentmann, der visuell vorging und dabei ‹goldene› und ‹silberne› Materialien miteinander in Beziehung setzte. Inwieweit bei dieser anderen Vorgehensweise die theoretische wissenschaftliche Arbeit durch die praktische Sammlungsarbeit zurück gedrängt wird ist leider nicht zu klären. Wichtig aber ist die Einsicht, dass ein Text nur eine Ordnung und Gliederung zulässt und diese festschreibt, wo hingegen Objekte immer wieder neu gruppiert und zueinander in Beziehung gesetzt werden können. Somit kann durch die variierende Präsentation der Materialien in der Sammlung im Gegensatz zur schriftlichen Abhandlung der wissenschaftliche Diskurs offen gehalten werden und immer wieder neue Sympathien und Ordnungskriterien generieren. Vor diesem Hintergrund interessant ist, dass Kentmann/Gesner zu Beginn des Mineralienkatalogs auf einer Doppelseite eine Abbildung des Sammelschrankes und eine tabellarische Präsentation seines Inhaltes bringen (Abb. 2 u. 3). Hier wird die enge Verbindung des eigentlichen Materials mit der Arbeit an seiner Ordnung und Kategorisierung, mit dem Ort seiner Präsentation sowie dem dazugehörigen Text deutlich hervorgehoben und alle diese Aspekte als gleichwertige Teile der wissenschaftlichen Erörterung betont.²⁹

Im Erzgebirge in und um St. Joachimsthal fließen um die Mitte des 16. Jahrhunderts die unterschiedlichen Aspekte der Materialforschung konstruktiv ineinander und beeinflussen sich gegenseitig. Das Sammeln, Kategorisieren und Deuten von Mineralen wird dabei durch eine vierte Gruppe von Akteuren mit ihren eigenen Praktiken und Methoden unterstützt. Es handelt sich um die Feinschmiede, die über Materialeigenschaften aus der eigenen Werkstatttätigkeit berichten können, und in deren Werk die Arbeiten der anderen drei ‹Forschergruppen› einfließen. Auch wenn sich keine aussagekräftigen schriftlichen Quellen erhalten haben, sind doch in dem St. Joachimsthaler Umfeld zwei Goldschmiedemeister zu rekonstruieren, deren Namen eng mit der Produktion von Handsteinen verbunden sind.³⁰ Es handelt sich dabei um Concz Welcz, der vor 1555 verstarb und Caspar Ulich, der möglicherweise aus der Werkstatt von Concz Welcz hervorging und bis zu seinem Tod 1576 dort tätig war.³¹ Die Chronica der Kayserlichern Freyen Bergstatt Sanct Joachimsthal berichtet zu diesem Jahr, dass der Goldschmied Caspar Ulich – «ein kunstreicher Meister auf allerley Ertzstuffen» am 18. Juli verstarb.³² Ulich stammte ursprünglich aus Zwickau und heiratete im Jahr 1555 die Witwe von Concz Welcz; 1575 hatte er das Amt des Stadtrichters inne.

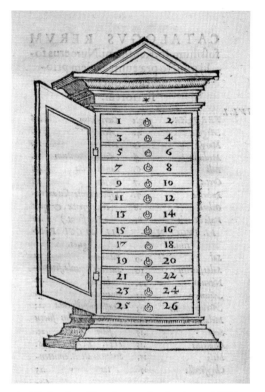

2/3 Johannes Kentmann, Graphische Darstellung des Inhalts seines Mineraliensammlerschrankes und Abbildung des Sammelschrankes, in: *De omni rerum fossilium genere, gemmis, lapidibus, metallis, et huiusmodi, libri aliquot, perique nun primi editi. Opera Conradi Gesneri*, Zürich 1566, S. 16 und 17.

Ein Jahr später, 1577, schreibt Kaiser Maximilian II. an die Böhmische Kammer:

> Wir fuegen euch genedigist zu wissen, das im Jochimstal ein goldschmidt, Caspar Ulrich genant; der hat ungeferlich sechszehn stuckh roch goldens erzt, so uns zusteet, bei seinen handen. Und weil wir dann solichs gerne haben wollten, so bevelhen wir euch demnach himit gnedigist, ir wellt unserm münzmaister daselbst im Joachimsthal an unser statt auferlegen, das er soliche stuckh ertz alsbals von ihm dem goldschmidt abfordern und sie euch unser Behaimbischen cammer zu handen wolverwart und also eingemacht, das sie nit schaden nehmen, schickhe, und wann ir die bekhommen habt, sie uns alsdann unverzüglich übersenden.[33]

Aus diesem Schreiben geht hervor, dass St. Joachimsthal und der dort tätige Goldschmied Caspar Ulich dem Kaiser bekannt waren, und er sich die Handsteine aus des Meisters Werkstatt für seine Sammlung sichern wollte. Die Verbindung von St. Joachimsthal und der Produktion von künstlerisch überarbeiteten Handsteinen ist ebenso durch Mathesius bestätigt, der in seiner 10. Hochzeitspredigt bemerkt, dass

> Gott lob in diesem thal viel schöner Historien, auß altem vnd newem Testament, auch auß erbarn und züchtigen Heydnischen Historien, auff schawgroschen gepreget und in ertz geschnitten sind [...] Ich köndte viel schöner groschen und stuffen erwehnen, die hie

im Tal zugericht, darinn neben trefflicher kunst, viel schöner artickel der wahren Religion zu sehen sindt...³⁴

Von Ruprecht Puellacher, einem weiteren Goldschmied und Münzmeister aus St. Joachimsthal, lässt sich kaum ein *oeuvre* nachweisen, dennoch gibt es eine in diesem Zusammenhang aussagekräftige Quelle zu seinem Wirken: seine Witwe verlangte im Jahr 1564 für den von ihrem Mann gefertigten Handstein von Kaiser Maximilian II. den Gegenwert von 7000 Talern.³⁵ Dieser wandte sich an seinen Bruder, den Erzherzog Ferdinand II., der als Kenner solcher Arbeiten den Wert des Handsteins schätzen sollte. Ferdinand antwortet in einem Schreiben vom 12. Juli 1565 dem Kaiser:

> nun manglt aber die Schaczung jeczo an dem, dass alhie im Behaim nit dergleichn Goltschmidt und Kunstler so mit solcher Arbeit umbzugehen, und sich darauf verstunden, vorhanden sein, und sollten das die Goldschmidt im Tall, die an denselben Hanndstain etlich Jarlang gearbeitet haben darzue erfordert worden, so ist zuebesorgen, Sie möchten solche in Kunst dermaßen hoch achten und scheczen, dass Euer Kay. Mt. u. Br. dieselb gaar zue theuer ankhomen wurde.³⁶

Ferdinand muss bekennen, dass die Schätzung bzw. der Vergleich des Wertes des Handsteins selbst ihm als Kenner der Materie nicht leicht fällt, da in Böhmen nur die Goldschmiede aus St. Joachimsthal diese Arbeiten auszuführen vermögen und so die Vergleichsbeispiele fehlten.

St. Joachimsthal erweist sich somit nicht nur als der Ort, an dem Erz abgebaut wird und daher Fachpersonal vorhanden ist; dieses Fachpersonal ist zudem Gesprächspartner von Gelehrten, die aus eigenem beruflichem Interesse – wie z.B. der Arzt Agricola – oder durch die eigene Sammlertätigkeit, wie Kentmann oder Mathesius, an mineralogischer Forschung beteiligt sind. Mathesius als Pfarrer von St. Joachimsthal ist darüber hinaus eine Art Vermittlerfigur, der als Chronist und Prediger Wissen verschriftlich, deutet und popularisiert. In diesem Umfeld inszenieren und überarbeiten die Goldschmiede besondere Erzstufen – dabei darf nicht vergessen werden, dass ihr *Experimentalwissen* über Schmelzpunkte, Formbarkeit, Dichte, Elastizität von Metallen, Legierungen etc. sicherlich auch in die wissenschaftlichen Traktate einfloss und darüber hinaus Impulse gab, solche experimentellen Methoden auch in die Mineralienforschung zu übernehmen.

Höfische Inszenierungen – die Metalle zwischen Natur und Kunst

Dieses gesammelte mineralogische Wissen konnte dann über die Erzstufen, sei es in ihrer natürlichen Form oder auch in dem von Goldschmieden gefassten Werk des Handsteins in die Kunstkammern überführt werden; dies aber ist nur eine von mehreren Möglichkeit, Bergthemen im Umfeld des Fürsten zu inszenieren. Ein anderer Weg war, die Handsteine in höfische Festumzüge zu integrieren: Kurfürst August von Sachsen führte 1574 beim Fastnachtsringen eine erste verbürgte bergmännische Invention auf.³⁷ Er präsentierte sich als Merkur, Gott der Metalle und Schutzherr des Bergbaus innerhalb einer Gruppe von Bergleuten, Hüttenarbeitern und Münzern und betonte damit sowohl sein landesherrliches Anrecht auf die aus dem Berg- und Münzregal erwachsenen Einnahmen, als auch seine Oberhoheit und Aufsichtspflicht über das gesamte Hüttenwesen. Im Zuge wurden *Blicksilber* und *Blickkupfer*, also besonders schöne Metallstufen mitgeführt, die deutlich auf die wirtschaftliche Bedeutung der sächsischen Montanindustrie verwiesen.

4   Daniel Bretschneider der Ältere, *Inventionen zum Ringrennen 1591*, Dresden, Sächsische Landesbibliothek, Mscr. Dresd. J 9.

Sein Nachfolger Kurfürst Christian I. erweiterte die Merkur-Invention 1591 durch zwei Wagen, die ein Schmelzofenmodell und ein Schaubergwerk vorführten. Der feuerspeiende Schmelzofenwagen mit Merkur präsentierte dabei die technischen Innovationen und die Leistungsfähigkeit der Montanindustrie wie das zweite Gefährt, auf dem Bergleute mit Schlägel und Eisen ein Bergwerk bevölkerten. Die Früchte dieser Arbeit wurden durch die mitgeführten Bergstufen in goldenen Schalen präsentiert, wobei zwei ungefasste Erze einen besonders prächtigen Handstein der oben von einem steigenden Einhorn bekrönt ist flankieren (Abb. 4). Als Schirmherren dieser Invention ritten Kurfürst Christian I. von Sachsen, Fürst Christian von Anhalt, der Oberhauptmann der Erzgebirge Heinrich von Schönberg sowie der kursächsische Berghauptmann Christoph von Schönberg in Bergmannstracht diesen Erzstufen voran.[38]

Weder die fürstliche Kunstkammer noch das Hofzeremoniell aber waren der Ort, wo bedeutungslose «wunderbarliche Gewechse von Metallen» aus reiner Freude am Bizarren versammelt wurden. Die hier vorgestellten Handsteine verweisen vielmehr über ihr Material deutlich auf den Bergbau und die damit verbundenen Themenfelder der mineralischen und metallurgischen Forschung sowie der Weiterentwicklung der Produktionsbedingungen innerhalb der Montanindustrie. Vincenzo Borghini formulierte programmatisch im Zusammenhang mit dem Studiolo von Francesco de' Medici im Palazzo Vecchio in Florenz: «Bedenkend das ähnliche Dinge nicht allein zur Natur und nicht allein zur Kunst gehören, sondern ihnen beide Teile eignen und dass das eine durch das andere gefördert wird…».

Als sprechendes Beispiel nennt er Diamanten, Rubine oder Kristalle, die die Natur nur in verunreinigtem Material gebe, das zudem noch «rozza» und «informe» wäre: Beide Worte deuten auf ein ‹Ungeformtsein› hin. Es sei nun Aufgabe der Kunst, die Steine zu reinigen und zu schneiden; als dritte Aufgabe der Kunst nennt er «riquadrare», indem das «Viereck» (quadro) enthalten ist, und das damit wiederum auf einen formgebenden künstlerischen Prozess hindeutet.[39]

Die kunsttheoretische Forderung der Zeit und der wissenschaftliche Erkenntnisanspruch mit Fokus auf Materialfragen treffen in den hier vorgestellten Objekten zusammen. Das agonale Verhältnis von Mensch/Natur bzw. Künstler/Kreator, das sich verkürzt im Dreisprung von ‹imitatio› (Nachahmung), von ‹aemulatio›

(Nacheiferung) und letztendlich der ‹superatio›, dem Übertreffung des natürlichen – und damit göttlichen – Schöpfungswerkes darstellen lässt, kann nicht mehr allein in der – mimetischen – Nachformung einer vorgebildeten Oberfläche erreicht werden, vielmehr muss der ‹artifex› ein inneres Verstehen der natürlichen Zusammenhänge und Strukturen anstreben.[40]

Die heute so oft als harmlose Kuriositäten klassifizierten Objekte hatten nicht vordergründig die Aufgabe, das Auge zu erfreuen und allgemeine Sympathien zwischen Mikro- und Makrokosmos augenscheinlich zu machen. Sie sind vielmehr hintergründige Objekte, geschaffen durch das ‹artificium› eines Feinschmieds, der Teil eines erfahrungsbasierten Gelehrten- und Praktiker-Netzwerkes war, das an der Verbesserung von mineralogischen, metallurgischen und montanistischen Kenntnissen arbeitete. Handsteine sind somit materialisiertes und daher auch inszenierbares empirisches Wissen, sie sind Ausstellungsstücke des landesherrlichen Bergbauregals und darüber hinaus Zeugnis für die künstlerische Auseinandersetzung mit den Schaffenskräften der Natur.

Anmerkungen

1 Barbara Gutfleisch und Joachim Menzhausen, «How a Kunstkammer should be formed. Gabriel Kaltemarckt's advice to Christian I of Saxony on the formation of an art collection, 1587», in: *Journal of the History of Collections*, 1989, Bd. 1, S. 3–32, hier S. 11.

2 Zu Handsteinen Julius von Schlosser, *Die Kunst- und Wunderkammern der Spätrenaissance. Ein Beitrag zur Geschichte des Sammelwesens*, Leipzig 1908, S. 50/51; Günther Schiedlausky, «Bergmännische Handsteine», in: *Der Anschnitt*, 1951, Bd. 3, Heft 5/6, S. 12–17; Peter Strieder, «Erzstufe», in: *Reallexikon zur deutschen Kunstgeschichte*, Band 5, Stuttgart 1967, Spalte 1408-1418; Werner Quellmalz, «Zur Materialfrage bergmännischer Handsteine der Renaissance. Untersuchungen eines Handsteins aus dem Grünen Gewölbe zu Dresden», in: *Der Anschnitt*, 1969, Bd. 21, Heft 1, S. 14–18; Rudolf Distelberger, «Gold und Silber, Edelsteine und Elfenbein», in: *Renaissance in Böhmen. Geschichte, Wissenschaft, Architektur, Plastik, Malerei, Kunsthandwerk*, hg. v. Ferdinand Seibt, München 1985, S. 255–287, hier S. 256–274; *Meisterwerke bergbaulicher Kunst vom 13. bis 19. Jahrhundert*, hg. v. Rainer Slotta und Christoph Bartels, Bochum 1990, Ausst. Kat. Deutsches Bergbau-Museum Bochum; Schloss Cappenberg, Kat. Nr. 244 a–k, S. 562–588; Stephan G. Storczer, *Die Handsteinsammlung des Kunsthistorischen Museums in Wien*, unveröffentlichte Diplomarbeit Universität Wien, März 1992; Peter Huber, «Die schönsten Stuffe. Handsteine aus fünf Jahrhunderten», in: *ExtraLapis*, 1995, Bd. 8, S. 58–67. *Bei diesem Schein kehrt Segen ein. Gold, Silber und Kupfer aus dem Slowakischen Erzgebirge*, hg. v. Rainer Slotte und Jürgen Labud, Bochum 1997, Ausst. Kat. Deutsches Bergbau-Museums Bochum, S. 122–135; Sven Dupré und Michael Korey, «Inside the Kunstkammer. The circulation of optical knowledge and instruments at the Dresden Court», in: *Studies in History and Philosophy of Science*, 2009, Bd. 40, S. 405–420.

3 Eine weitere Sonderform sind vollständig künstliche Handsteine, bei denen aus unterschiedlichen Mineralen bergartige Gebilde geschaffen wurden, die wiederum als eine Art Bühne für meist biblische Szenen dienten, wie z. B. die Doppelscheuer mit Handstein in einer Kokosnuss aus dem Kunsthistorischen Museum in Wien, Inv. Nr. 885/886, Strocer 1992 (wie Anm. 2), Kat. Nr. 1, S. 68–71.

4 Ebd., Bd. 1, S. 97–100: Das Monogramm des Künstlers (ligiertes CV) findet sich auf beiden Stein der Silberstufe; Gesamthöhe des Objektes ist 31,7 cm, wobei der Fuß (mit den vier Wappenschilden, die den Reichsadler, den Tirol Adler sowie die Wappen von Ungarn und Böhmen zeigen) 10,8 cm hoch, der Handstein 20,9 cm hoch ist.

5 Der Vater von Erzherzog Ferdinand II. (1529–1595), Kaiser Ferdinand I. (1503–1654) erbte durch seine Heirat mit der Jagiellonin Anna (1503–1547) die Königswürde von Ungarn und Böhmen nach dem Tod von Annas Bruder, Ludwig II. (1506–1526). Ferdinand II. wurde nach der Schlacht bei Mühlberg 1547 als Statthalter im Königreich Böhmen eingesetzt; den Grundstein für seine Sammlung in Schloss Ambras scheint er in jenen Jahren gelegt zu haben; nach dem Tod seines Vaters wurde Ferdinand II. 1564 Erzherzog von Tirol und übersiedelt nach Innsbruck; in diese Zeit fällt der Ausbau von Schloss Ambras, wo Ferdinands Gemahlin Philippine Welser wohnte. Alfred Auer, «Erzherzog Ferdinand II. Renaissancefürst und Herr über Rüstkammern, Kunstkammer und Bibliothek auf Schloss Ambras», in: *Natur und Kunst. Handschriften und Alben aus der Ambraser Sammlung Erzherzog Ferdinands II. (1529–1595)*, hg. v. Alfred Auer und Eva Irblich, Wien 1995, Ausst. Kat. Kunsthistorisches Museum Wien und Österreichische Nationalbibliothek, S. 13–19. Zur Sammlung an sich *Die Kunstkammer. Kunsthistorisches Museum Sammlungen Schloß Ambras*, bearb. v. Elisabeth Scheicher, Innsbruck 1977, (Führer durch das KHM 27); Elisabeth Scheicher, «The collection af Archduke Ferdinand II. at Schloss Ambras. Its purpose, composition and evolution», in: *The origins of Museums. The Cabinet of Curiosities in Sixteenth and Seventeenth-Century Europe*, hg. v. Oliver Impey und Arthur MacGregor, Oxford 1985, S. 29–38; *Alle Wunder dieser Welt. Die kostbarsten Kunstwerke aus der Sammlung Erzherzog Ferdinands II. (1529–1595)*, hg. v. Wilfried Seipel, Wien 2001, Ausst. Kat. Kunsthistorische Sammlungen Schloss Ambras, 2001; *Die Entdeckung der Natur. Naturalien in den Kunstkammern des 16. und 17. Jahrhunderts*, hg. v. Wilfried Seipel, Wien 2006, Ausst. Kat. Schloss Ambras und Kunsthistorisches Museum Wien, 2006.

6 Das Inventar der Kunstkammer vom 30. Mai 1595, gegeben in Innsbruck, ist unter der Nr. 5556, S. CCLVIII–CCCXIII ediert in: «Urkunden und Regesten aus der k.k. Hofbibliothek. Teil 1», hg. v. Wendelin Boeheim, in: *Jahrbuch der kunsthistorischen Sammlungen des Allerhöchsten Kaiserhauses*, 1888, Bd. 7, S. XCI-CCCXIII (Quellen zur Geschichte der kaiserlichen Haussammlungen und der Kunstbestrebungen des Allerdurchlauchtigsten Erzhauses); der Inhalt des Dritten Kastens mit den Handsteinen findet sich auf S. CCLXXXIII–CCLXXXV; Der Inhalt der Bibliothek ediert in: «Urkunden und Regesten aus der k.k. Hofbibliothek. Teil 2», hg. v. Wendelin Boeheim, in: *Jahrbuch der* *kunsthistorischen Sammlungen des Allerhöchsten Kaiserhauses*, 1889, Bd. 10 (Quellen zur Geschichte der kaiserlichen Haussammlungen und der Kunstbestrebungen des Allerdurchlauchtigsten Erzhauses), S. I–X, wo auf S. IV leider nur summarisch der auf den fol. 641–643 aufgelistete Inhalt des Tisches, mit Erzen aus St. Joachimsthal, Falkenstein, Villach und Handsteine, genannt wird; Margot Rauch, «Steinreich. Gesammeltes aus der Erde», in: Seipel 2006 (wie Anm. 5), S. 157–158, hier S. 158: Der Sammeltisch, Inv. Nr. PA 141, ist eines der ältesten erhaltenen Museumsmöbel. Die 41 Handsteine in der Kunstkammer waren künstlerisch überarbeitet, die Handsteine im Bibliothekstisch hingegen im natürlichen Zustand belassen. Vgl. auch Gerhard Niedermayr, «Erzherzog Johann und Schloss Ambras», in: *Kaiser, König, Kieselstein*, hg. v. Johannes Keilmann, München 1996, S. 58–65, (Offizieller Katalog der 33. Mineralientage München 1.–3. November 1996. Messethemenheft).

7 «... In dem gebirg aber, wo gediegen silber oder rotguldenerz gebrochen wird, sollt ihr fleissig nachsehen lassen, damit uns ein schöner handstein, ob er schon einen halben centner schwer, mit samt dem so damit auch dabei, daben und darumben stehend es sei an erz und gebirg gebrochen und fürder mit allem fleiss eingemacht und durch einen eigenen boten hiehergeschickt.» in: *Entbieten und Befehl*, Tiroler Landesarchiv, Innsbruck, 1574, fol. 451, zitiert nach Josphen Hirn, *Erzherzog Ferdinand II. von Tirol. Geschichte seiner Regierung und seiner Länder*, Innsbruck 1887, Band 2, Kapitel III: Ambras, S. 421–449, hier S. 438.

8 Besonders große und formschöne Funde kamen häufig als Geschenk der Bergverwaltung an den Landesherren; 1880 wurden 68 Mineralien aus der Ambraser Sammlung in das k. k. Naturhistorische Hofmuseum übertragen, darunter auch ein Stephanit und ein Argentit aus St. Joachimsthal, dazu Seipel 2006 (wie Anm. 5), Kat. Nr. 3.7. und Kat. Nr. 3.8, S. 163/164. Dort auch (Kat. Nr. 3.10) ein Zinnstein aus Schlaggenwald. Alle drei Stücke befinden sich heute im Naturhistorischen Museum in Wien, in der Mineralogisch-Petrographischen Abteilung. Vgl. auch Georg Gebhard, «Minerale als Symbole der Macht», in: Keilmann 1996 (wie Anm. 6), S. 28–35.

9 Die Nürnberger Patrizierfamilie Scheurl hatte auch einen Handstein von 1563, und diese Familie besaß beträchtliche Anteile an Bergwerken in Schlackenwald und St. Joachimsthal, dazu Ernst Günther Troche, «Die Erzstufe des Christoph III. Scheurl», in: *Jahresbericht Germanisches Nationalmuseum Nürnberg*, 1950, Bd. 95, S. 15–23, hier S. 16–18.

10 Harald Marx, «Bergbau und Kunst in Sachsen», in: *Der silberne Boden. Kunst und Bergbau in Sachsen*, hg. v. Manfred Bachmann, Harald Marx und Eberhard Wächtler, Leipzig 1990, Ausst. Kat. Albertinum an der Brühlschen Terrasse 1989, S. 9–16, hier S. 12, nach der Beschreibung der Kunstkammer durch Tobias Beutel, *Churfürstlicher Sächsischer stets grünender hoher Cedernwald auf dem grünen Rauten-Grunde oder kurtze Vorstellung d. chur-fürstl. sächs. hohen Regal-Wercke nehmlich: Der Fürtrefflichen Kunst-Kammer und anderer Seiner Chur-Fürstl. Durchl. hochschätzbaren unvergleich wichtigen Dinge allhier by der Residenz Dresden ... gantz kürtzlich in lateinischer und teutscher Sprache beschrieben ... von Tobias Beutelnn*, Dresden 1671, o.S. Siehe auch Klaus Thalheim, «... aus hiesigen Land-Ertz zusammen gesetzt. Mineralogische Kostbarkeiten aus der Schatzkammer der Sächsischen Kurfürsten in Dresden» in: Keilmann 1996 (wie Anm. 6), S. 72–80. Gerhard Mathé, «Mineralogische und geologische Sammlungen», in: Bachmann u.a. 1990 (wie Anm. 10), S. 457: «In dem ersten sächsischen Kunstkammer-Inventarium, das Kurfürst Christian I 1587 anfertigen ließ, waren bereits einige Minerale und Gesteine aus sächsischen Vorkommen verzeichnet, allerdings noch immer keine solchen aus erzgebirgischen Silberlagerstätten. Diese tauchen erst in den Inventaren von 1595 und 1610 auf und werden im Verlaufe des 17. Jahrhunderts den kurfürstlichen Sammlungen in verstärktem Maße zugeführt.

11 1587 schenkte Christian I. von Sachsen sieben Erzstufen, die zuvor in der Rentkammer verwahrt worden waren, seiner Gemahlin Sophia; fünf dieser Handsteine waren «von gewachsenem Silber-, Glas- und rothgolden Erz» und zeigten biblische Geschichten, der sechste Handstein zeigte einen Bergmann, der siebte war «von allerlei Bergarten» zusammengesetzt. Theodor Diestel, «Handsteine Kurfürst Christians I. von Sachsen», in: *Zeitschrift für Museologie und Antiquitätenkunde sowie für verwandte Wissenschaften*, 1882, Bd. 5, Heft 1, S. 4.

12 Lothar Klapper, *Vom Altbergbau. Von den Anfängen bis zu seiner Blüte im 16. Jahrhundert*, Annaberg 2002, (Beiträge zur Geschichte des Landkreises Annaberg 2), S. 30–56.

13 Adalbert Wrany, *Die Pflege der Mineralogie in Böhmen. Ein Beitrag zur vaterländischen Geschichte der Wissenschaften*, Prag 1896, v.a. S. 1–29; Volker Schmidtchen, «Technik im Übergang vom Mittelalter zur Neuzeit zwischen 1350 und 1600», in: Karl-Heinz Ludwig und Volker Schmidtchen, *Metalle und Macht 1000 bis 1600*, Berlin 1992, (Propyläen Technikgeschichte 2), S. 209–598, hier v.a. S. 209–246.

14 Friedrich Naumann, «450 Jahre ‹De re metallica libri XII›. Das Hauptwerk Georgius Agricolas», in: *Von Georgius Agricola zum Mitteldeutschen Braunkohlenbergbau. Aspekte der Montangeschichte*, hg. v. Hans-Joachim Braun, Freiberg

2006, (Die Technikgeschichte als Vorbild moderner Technik 31), S. 13–44; Walther Fischer, «Agricola, der Vater der Mineralogie», in: *Georg Agricola 1494–1555 zu seinem 400. Todestag 21. November 1955,* hg. v. Georg Spackeler, Berlin 1955, S. 66–80; Jiri Majer, «Ore Mining and the Town of St. Joachimsthal/Jachymov at the Time of Georgius Agricola», in: *GeoJournal,* 1994, Bd. 32, S. 91–99.

15 1557 folgte eine deutsche Übersetzung (Vom Bergkwerck XII Bücher), in Basel durch Philipp Bech, dazu Beat Rudolf Jenny, «Die Übersetzung von Agricolas ‹De re metallica› als Beispiel für die Verbreitung wissenschaftlicher Texte in der Landessprache des 16. Jahrhunderts», in: *Ferrum,* 1995, Bd. 67, S. 16–25.

16 Zum Gelehrtenkreis um Agricola zählen desweiteren Bartholomäus Bach, 1530 Berggegenschreiber in St. Joachimsthal und Petrus Plateanus, Lateinschulrektor und Herausgeber des Bermannus, Wrany 1896 (wie Anm. 13), S. 6; Naumann 2006 (wie Anm. 14), S. 19.

17 Georg Agricola, *Bermannus oder über den Bergbau. Ein Dialog,* übers. und bearb. v. Helmut Wilsdorf, Hans Prescher und Heinz Techel, Berlin 1955, (Georgius Agricola. Ausgewählte Werke 2), S. 165

18 Agricola erklärt in der Widmung zu *De natura fossilium,* dass die heimischen Bergwerke nicht alle Fossiliengattungen erzeugen, er sich daher darum bemühte, dass Fehlende nicht nur aus allen Gegenden Deutschlands, sondern auch aus allen Bergewerken Europas, aber auch Asiens und Afrikas zu erhalten und ausspricht, dass ihn Bergleute, Gelehrte und Kaufleute bei seiner Arbeit mit ihren Mitteilungen unterstützt haben.

19 Johannes Mathesius, *Chronika der Keyserlichen Freyen Bergstadt Sanct Joachimsthal, der zuvor die Conradsgrün genennt war* erschien im Anschluss an die *Sarepta,* Nürnberg 1564. Karl Siegl, *Die Joachimsthaler Chronik (des Johannes Mathesius) von 1516–1617 mit einer Lebensgeschichte des Joh. Mathesius als Einleitung,* St. Joachimsthal 1923. Zu Mathesius: Georg Loesche, «Johannes Mathesius», in: *Die Wunderstadt St. Joachimsthal. Eine Monographie,* hg. v. Karl Knopf, Band 6, Weipert/Leipzig 1909, S. 55–127. Zu seiner überregionalen Mineraliensammlung schreibt Mathesius: «Von der Eul in Behem, wie auch aus den Ungerischen Bergstedten, und etlichen Steyerischen gebirgen, sind mir etliche goldstüfflein, und schöne wörflete marchasith, gelff und agstein, der in Fletzten nierig, zu Leinbach in Oesterreich jetzt bricht, zukommen, wie mir auss der Rauriess unnd Gastein vil seltzamer bergart zugeschickt, dergleichen Doctor Agricola, wie er in meinem hauss frey bekennt, zuvor nie gesehen. Auss Schwatz im Inthal bin ich mit Federweiss un schönen Malachiten versehen, vom Stalberg auss der Pfaltz mit einem schönen kiss, darinn queck oder weich silber gestanden. Man hat mich auch mit Gosslarischem pleyertz, gelb, grau astramenti, natürlichem und getroffnem Vitriol, unnd von Mansfeld mit schönen schifern, darinn Fisch sehr ercklich mit kupffer überzogen, gebilet gewsen, versorget. Ich hab auch vom Graupen eine weisse Zinngraupe, un von Schlackenwald, sehr schönen durchsichtigen spat, darinn kiss und zwitter gestanden, und von den Platten allerley Farben zingraupen, blutstein, glasskopff, und die schönsten Flüss, neben einer ehrlichen verehrung von zin zum Haussrath. Item von Schwartzenburg und Caffen sehr gute Magneten bekommen.»

20 Heribert Sturm, *Die St. Joachimsthaler Lateinschulbibliothek aus dem 16. Jahrhundert,* Stuttgart 1964 (Forschungen zur Geschichte und Landeskunde der Sudentenländer 4), über die Rolle von Mathesius beim Aufbau der Bibliothek der St. Joachimsthaler Lateinschule, deren Rektor er seit 1532 war, v.a. S. 4–24. Im Widmungsschreiben vom 1. Dezember 1550 an den sächsischen Fürsten formuliert Agricola, dass er durch angeworbene Zeichner habe Abbildungen schaffen lassen, «damit die mit Worten beschriebenen Dinge, die den gegenwärtigen und zukünftigen Menschen unbekannt sind, ihnen keine Schwierigkeiten für das Verständnis bereiten». Mathesius war bei der Vermittlung der Zeichner (namentlich Basilius Wefring aus St. Joachimsthal) behilflich, Wilhelm Pieper, «Die kunstgeschichtliche Stellung und die illustrationstechnische Bedeutung der Holzschnitte in Agricolas ‹De re Metallica›», in: Spackeler 1955 (wie Anm. 14), S. 266–291, hier S. 274.

21 *Sarepta* 1564 (wie Anm. 19), S. LXXXVI verso und LXXXVII.

22 Wolfgang Sommer, «Gottes Odem in der Schöpfung. Zum Bild der Natur bei Johan Arndt und Jakob Böhme», in: Wolfgang Sommer, *Politik, Theologie und Frömmigkeit im Luthertum der Frühen Neuzeit. Ausgewählte Aufsätze,* Göttingen 1999, S. 206–227. Zum Buch der Natur Hans Blumenberg, *Die Lesbarkeit der Welt,* Frankfurt/Main 1979; Heribert M. Nobis, «Buch der Natur», in: *Historisches Wörterbuch der Philosophie,* Band 1, hg. v. Joachim Ritter, Darmstadt 1971, Sp. 957–959; Erich Rothacker, *Das ‹Buch der Natur›. Materialien und Grundsätzliches zur Metapherngeschichte,* Bonn 1979.

23 *Sarepta* 1564 (wie Anm. 19), S. LXXXVII.

24 *Sarepta* 1564 (wie Anm. 19), S. LXXXVIII recto. Die gleiche Stufe wird auch in der 10. Hochzeitspredigt kurz erwähnt: Johannes Mathesius, *Hochzeitspredigten,* hg. v. Georg Loesche, Prag 1897, (Ausgewählte Werke 2), S. 179/180. Das Stück wird ebenso im Nachlassinventar von Schloss Ambras von 1596 ausführlich beschrieben, gehörte also nachweislich in den Besitz von Erzherzog Ferdinand, Urkunden 1888, S. CCLXXXIV, fol. 365v: «Mer ain schöner geschnitner handstain wie ain perg von glaszärzt, daran ain kaiserliche fügur mit seinem scepter und cron auf dem kopf und ain kinigliche person, vor dem kaiser knieend, oben an dem perg daz kaiserliche wappen mit den zwo seilen, steet auf einem silbern ganz vergulten fuesz, daran das kaiserlich, Beheimisch, Unngrisch und Tirolisch wappen geschmeltz, auf der andern seiten die urstend Christi von geschnitnem galsärzt.»

25 Johannes Helm, *Johannes Kentmann 1518–1574. Ein sächsischer Arzt und Naturforscher*, Wiesbaden 1971, (Sudhoffs Archiv Beiheft 13).

26 Hans Prescher, «Von Sammlern und Sammlungen des Mineralreiches im 16. Jahrhunderts», in: Spackeler 1955 (wie Anm. 14), S. 320–338, hier S. 320, gibt einen Überblick über die wichtigsten Sammler des 16. und frühen Jahrhunderts (Aricola, Mathesius, Kentmann, Gesner, Ferdinand II. von Tirol, Anselmus Boetius de Boodt und Nosseni).

27 *De omni rerum fossilium genere, gemmis, lapidibus, metallis, et huiusmodi, libri aliquot, perique nun primi editi. Opera Conradi Gesneri*, Zürich 1566; darin enthalten *Io. Kentmani Dresdensis Medici Nomenclaturae Rerum fossilium, quae in Misnia praecipue & in aliis quoque regionibus inveniuntur*, auf den Seiten 16–95v; Georgius Agricola. *Bergwelten 1494–1994*, hg. v. Bern Ernsting, Essen 1994, S. 263, Ausst. Kat. Schloßbergmuseum Chemnitz/Deutsches Bergbau-Museum Bochum, 1994.

28 Gesner/Kentmann 1566 (wie Anm. 27), S. 60r (S. 141), «13. Repertum in Valle Ioachimica in ligno abiegno. Auff S. Lorenz in Jochimsthal in Thennenholz gewachsen. 14. Annebergium candidum capilare, rude, rubrum, pellucidum item rude plumbei coloris in uno lapide distinctum et coniunctum. Ein handstein darinn häricht silber durchsichtig roth gulden ertz und glaß ertz zu gleych unterschiedlich.»

29 Ebd., S. 16 und 17; bei der tabellarischen Präsentation sind die einzelnen Fächer von 1–26 jeweils mit dem Inhalt bezeichnet (von «1. Terrae» bis «26. Marina Varia»); auf der gegenüberliegenden Seite folgt dann die Abbildung des tatsächlichen Schrankens, bei dem auf die Schubfächer des Möbels die entsprechenden Zahlen aufgetragen sind.

30 Heribert Sturm, «Alt-Joachimsthaler Kunstgewerbe», in: *Deutsche Heimat*, 1933, Bd. 9, S. 166–169 (Wiederabdruck in Heribert Sturm, *Skizzen zur Geschichte des Obererzgebirges im 16. Jahrhundert. Forschungen zur Geschichte und Landeskunde der Sudetenländer*, München 1965, (Veröffentlichungen der Historischen Kommission der Sudentenländer 5), S. 46–47.

31 Edmund Wilhelm Braun, «Concz Welcz, der Goldschmied zu St. Joachimsthal», in: *Kunst und Kunsthandwerk*, 1917, Bd. 20, S. 422–429; Edmund Wilhelm Braun, «Weitere signierte Arbeiten des Joachimsthaler Goldschmiedes Concz Welcz», in: *Kunst und Kunsthandwerk*, 1920, Bd. 23, S. 212–216.

32 *Bergpostilla, oder Sarepta, darinn von allerley Bergkwerck und Metallen, was ir Eygenschaft und Natur, und wie sie zu Nutz und Gut gemacht, guter Bericht gegeben wird*, Nürnberg, 1578. Darin: *Chronica der Kayserlichen Freyen Bergstatt Sanct Joachimsthal* [Fortführung der Chronik von Johannes Mathesius], S. 629.

33 Walther Fischer, «Kaiser Rudolf II., Mineraliensammler und Mäzen der Edelsteinbearbeitung», in: *Der Aufschluss*, 1971, Bd. 22, S. 1–36, hier S. 2.

34 Mathesius 1897 (wie Anm. 24), S. 169–190: «Die zehende Hochzyt Prdigt von dem alten Goldarbeiter und Steinschneider Bezalelle», hier S. 186.

35 Archiv des Ministeriums des Inneren (heute Österreichisches Staatsarchiv), Kopialbuch 75, fol. 113–114, zitiert nach Viktor Katz, *Die erzgebirgische Prägemedaille des 16. Jahrhunderts*, Prag 1932, S. 11, Fußnote 2.

36 Ebd., S. 11, Anmerkung 2; zitiert aus *Archiv des Ministeriums des Innern* (wohl heute Österreichisches Staatsarchiv), Kopialbuch 79, fol. 236–237 und fol. 52r/v.

37 Jutta Bäumel, «Die Darstellung des Bergbaus im höfischen Fest des 16. und 17. Jahrhunderts», in: Brachmann u.a. 1990 (wie Anm. 10), S. 213–219.

38 Die Zeichnung stammt von Daniel Bretschneider dem Älteren und wird in Dresden, Sächsische Landesbibliothek, MScr. Dresd. J 9 verwahrt.

39 Vincenzo Borghini, *Inventione per Sua Altezza, stanzini. Florenz 1570, Lo Zibaldone di Giorgio Vasari*, hg. v. Alessandro De Vita, Arezzo 1938, S. 47–51: «... considerando che simil cose non son tutte della natura né tutte dell'arte, ma vi hanno ambedue parte, aiutandosi l'una all'altra [come per dare un esempio la natura da il suo diamante, o carbonchio o cristallo, et riunite altra materia rozza et informe, et l'arte gli pulisce, riquarda, intaglia, atcetera, però havea pensato che tuta questa inventione fosse dedicta alla natura et all'arte [...]. Et però nel tondo del mezzo che è nel chielo sarà dipinta la natura che harà in compagnia sua Prometheo ...»; siehe auch Luigi Salerno, «Arte, Scienza e Collezioni nel Manierismo», in: *Scritti di Storia dell'Arte in onore di Mario Salmi (Terzo Volume)*, Rom 1963, S. 194–214, hier bes. S. 199–200; *Der literarische Nachlaß Giorgio Vasaris*, hg. v. Karl Frey und Hermann-Walther Frey, Bd. 2, München 1930, S. 887 übersetzt: «... in Anbetracht dessen, daß derartige Dinge [...] nicht alle der Natur oder der Kunst angehören, sondern beide daran beteiligt sind, da sie einander helfen, wie, um ein Beispiel anzuführen, die Natur den Diamanten oder den Karfunkel oder den Kristall gemischt mit anderem frohen, unförmigem Stoff liefert und die Kunst sie säubert, schleift und graviert [...], habe ich daher gedacht, daß diese *inventione* ganz der Natur und der Kunst gewidmet sein soll [...], und deshalb soll in dem Medaillon in der Mitte des Himmels die Natur in Begleitung von Prometheus abgebildet sein etc.»

40 Einführend zum Begriff der ‹aemulatio› Jan-Dirk Müller und Ulrich Pfisterer, «Der allgegenwärtige Wettstreit in den Künsten der Frühen Neuzeit», in: *Aemulatio. Kulturen des Wettstreits in Text und Bild (1450–1629)*, hg. v. Jan-Dirk Müller u.a., Berlin/Boston 2011, S. 1–32; Kristine Patz, «Manierismus VII. Bildende Kunst», in: *Historisches Wörterbuch der Rhetorik*, Bd. 5, Tübingen, 2001, Sp. 907–920; Gerhard Wolf, «Gestörte Kreise. Zum Wahrheitsanspruch des Bildes im Zeitalter des Disegno», in: *Räume des Wissens. Repräsentation, Codierung, Spur*, hg. v. Hans-Jörg Rheinberger, Michael Hagner und Bettina Schmidt-Wahrig, Berlin 1997, S. 39–62.

Joris van Gastel
Geology and Imagery in the Kingdom of Naples:
A Letter on the Origins of Alabaster (1696)

On the 28th of January 1696, the Salernitan *letterato* Simone Barra sent out a long overdue letter to his friend Filippo Bulifon in Naples.[1] Apologizing for his failure to comply with the duties of friendship, Barra recounts how he has decided to break the silence with an account of «that which during a small trip from Capriati I have seen in a cave, where flowing water changes into the hardest of stones».[2] In 1698, Filippo's father Antonio Bulifon published the letter in the fourth volume of his *Lettere memorabili*, a collection of letters that encompasses topics as varied as politics, literature, medicine, geology, and natural history. And even if Barra's contribution fits in well with other letters that discuss the «generation of pearls», «Mount Vesuvius and its fires», and the «phenomena that are seen at the mountain of the sulphur mines near Pozzuoli», it differs from these accounts due to the author's unique literary approach.[3] The resulting text is a highly interesting document on material aesthetics and geology, giving an indication of how material associations were shaped between art, science, and poetry. Pamela Smith has argued that in early modern Europe «the things of nature and their verbal and visual representations were constitutive of communities of artists, collectors, and naturalists», and that these communities, in turn, «shaped disciplines and created knowledge».[4] Barra's letter can be seen as a trace of such processes, shedding light on some of the debates involved.

Around Aurora's Table

About Barra we know little. He is mentioned in passing by Bernardo De Dominici in his *Vite dei pittori, scultori, ed architetti napolitani* of 1742, where the author relates that Barra was in fact well-known among the *letterati* of his time and that he worked until old age as secretary to Duchess D. Aurora Sanseverino di Laurenzano, wife to Nicolò Gaetani dell'Aquila d'Aragona.[5] Other sources indicate that he would later become a member of the literary academy of the *Caprario*, established in 1728 by Francesco Carafa, prince of Colobrano.[6] His literary output, however, as far as it has been published, is confined to a handful of poems, one of which appears on the first page of another of Bulifon's volumes of *Lettere memorabili*, and of course the letter to Filippo Bulifon.[7] Barra's investigative nature is further confirmed by a much later source. In his *Dissertazioni istoriche delle antichità alifane* of 1776, Gianfranceso Trutta recounts that he had heard from his older brother Marzio, elsewhere described as a collector and lover of antiquities, how he, together with the «*celebre letterato* Simone Barra of Salerno» and several others had descended into a dark, underground ruin in the city of Alife, lighting their way with torches.[8]

Much more is known about Barra's employer, Aurora Sanseverino. Among the first female members of the Accademia dell'Arcadia, she was deeply involved with poetry. Moreover, she was a patron of the arts and played an important role in the early developments of the opera.[9] She promoted some lesser known Neapolitan artists too, including De Dominici, who writes in his *Vite* that he had worked for the Duchess as a landscape painter. Inventories of the dwellings in Naples and Piedimonte indicate that she and her husband brought together important art collections. In fact, De Dominici mentions a number of works, including a *Saint Andrew* by Giuseppe de Ribera, «impastato a maraviglia», and from the hand of Salvator Rosa «two landscapes, not very large, with stones reflecting in the water, tree trunks, and a hermit [*romito*] in both, [painted] with a marvellous touch, as well as two ovals with rocks and figures, only sketched».[10]

Worthy of mention is also the elaborate salt cellar described by De Dominici, that, «to inspire wonder and delight», adorned the centre of the large table to which Aurora invited her many guests. Made by the Neapolitan goldsmith Gian Domenico Vinaccia after a design by his compatriot the painter Luca Giordano, it measured more than five *palmi* (1.32 meters) in height and was made up of a large number of figures to create an intricate iconographic program.[11] As Vinaccia died in 1695, shortly after his completion of the extraordinary *paleotto* adorning the main altar of the Cappella di San Gennaro, the salt cellar must have been made before this date.[12] Hence, it was right there on the table when Barra wrote his letter. From De Dominici's description, it is difficult to determine whether the figures adorning the show-piece relate in any explicit way to the salt it contained; with figures of the four parts of the world, the times of the day, time itself in the figure of Saturn, and personifications of glory and immortality pointing out the temple of eternity that topped the whole construction, the salt cellar contained almost a microcosm in itself. That salt could be very much seen as a part of such a cosmos, may follow from the work of the German scholar Johann Rudolf Glauber, who, in his *Tractatus de natura salium* of 1658, not only praises the virtues of ordinary table salt, but sees salt as the foundational element of all things, even concluding that it is no less than a symbol of eternity.[13] In any case, the striking structure cannot but have been brought into connection with the very earthly mineral it contained, and thus art and geology come here together at the centre of the table where both must have been eagerly debated.[14] Through his employer, then, Barra was right in the midst of such debates, a fact which is also borne out by his letter.

Feverish Dreams

When describing his approach to the grotto, Barra sketches an idyllic, indeed almost Arcadian, landscape. His elaborate descriptions of the flow of the river Lete, containing «more trout than waves», and the thick wood of extraordinary cypress trees topping the hill, suggest a profound interest in the world that surrounds him. It is a companion, however, who draws his attention to the cave, carved out of «fine and bright» alabaster. They enter the grotto with lights. Even the grotto itself has nothing of the terrifying character usually associated with natural phenomena of its kind.[15] Rather, Barra is struck by the wonderful patterns and shapes he discovers here.

It is this decorative quality of the material that also fascinated contemporaries. Although a lesser known sculptor such as Antonio Giorgetti might carve the occasional portrait bust from alabaster, the material was more readily incorporated in architecture and applied art, where it was praised for decorative qualities that sometimes verged on the figurative.[16] A striking example of such an appreciation can be found in a seventeenth-century description of the Ginetti chapel in the Roman church of Sant'Andrea della Valle:

> [the lantern] has in its summit a beautiful tangle of clouds, but without the use of any brush, represented true to life in pure alabaster, contrived thus, that at the same instant it deceives and consoles the sense of sight.[17]

The striking patterns in the veined stone, as well as its translucence, made it in itself a spectacle worthy of notice. The painterly qualities of the stone must have played a role also in the practice of using alabaster as a support for painting by artists such as Hans von Aachen around the turn of the previous century. Even if this practice seems to have been popular only for a brief period, paintings of this kind did abound in important art collections.[18] Barra might, for example, have been familiar with the anonymous picture «painted on alabaster, with the Virgin and Child, Saint Joseph and Saint John, in an ebony frame», mentioned together with a painting of the Ship of Saint Peter on agate in the Neapolitan collection of Elisabetta Vandeneynden and Carlo Carafa.[19] The most popular application of the material, however, seems to have been for vases or urns, of which large numbers are mentioned in contemporary inventories.

Returning to Barra's letter, we get a taste of the whimsical character of the shapes produced in stone:

> …the walls of the cave [were] full of those before mentioned outgrowths or lumps that, carved in low relief, exhibited the strangest ramifications and figures, [so strange indeed,] that Michelangelo would not have been able to invent them in his drawing of the Roman grotesques.[20]

With its wealth of images shaped by nature, the cave was just one example of the figurative powers of stone, a topic that was much debated in the period.[21] In his *Mundus subterraneus* of 1664 the Jesuit scholar Athanasius Kircher devoted a whole chapter to figures emerging in stone, providing examples ranging from characters to animals to whole biblical scenes. For his compendium, Kircher relied on the collection he had brought together at the Collegio Romano. However, the images reproduced in the book are largely derived from the illustrations in Ulisse Aldrovandi's *Musaeum metallicum*, a taxonomic work on geology published posthumously in 1648 and grounded in his own collection in Bologna.[22]

Barra's association of the grotesque with Michelangelo is somewhat puzzling. Even if some sources do suggests such an association, it is more likely that Barra simply combined the name of a well-known artist with a well-known phenomenon.[23] Closer to home, Barra might have been thinking of the rich incrustations that adorn so many seventeenth-century chapels and altars in Neapolitan churches. Characterized by grotesque-like patterns in large varieties of marble and precious stones, often meticulously described in the contracts, they gained their most exuberant expression in the hands of the sculptor and architect Cosimo Fanzago.[24] For one author, these incrustations appeared to be «painted rather than sculpted».[25]

However, as another account of a visit to a cave illustrates—written by Giovanni Battista Francolo and published in Ireneo della Croce's *Historia della città di Trieste*, it came out in the same year as Barra's letter—the shapes found in grottoes could be very much sculptural, or even architectural:

the streams of waters have turned into stone, and with the marvellous artifice of nature itself, have arranged themselves in the guise of well shaped columns, festoons, garlands of flowers and fruits, and other similar artful things, that fill the beholder with marvel and surprise.[26]

And yet, these wondrous shapes formed by nature were not in themselves what impressed Barra. What seems to have impressed him the most, was the fact that he saw them coming into being right before his eyes. The dripping water, he writes,

...has resulted in transfigurations so new, [...] that in that moment it seemed to me that I saw all of the metamorphoses of Ovid. There Daphne half changed into laurel with the eager Apollo right behind, there the doleful Niobe hardened into cold stone with streams of living tears running from her eyes, and the miserable fate of the youngster Acis one could observe, with the copious water running like sweat from all over his body, showing him to turn subtly into a river. And many, many more were the images produced by this enchanted cave, every single one inimitable by the human imagination.[27]

With his allusion to Ovid's *Metamorphoses*, Barra conjures up not only this ancient text but also some of the most evocative literary and artistic images of the *Seicento*. The story of the nymph Daphne, for whom the only way to escape her assailant Apollo was to be turned into a laurel tree, has no more iconic image than Gian Lorenzo Bernini's marble sculpture in the Villa Borghese, while the sculpture, in turn, is deeply embedded in contemporary poetry.[28] Niobe, who out of grief for her slain children turned to marble though never ceased to weep, was understood as the epitome of sorrow and functioned as such for the Neapolitan poet Giambattista Marino in his *Strage degli innocenti*, a poetic interpretation of the biblical Massacre of the Innocents.[29] The Bolognese painter Guido Reni turned to the famous antique sculpture of Niobe in the garden of the Villa Medici for one of the mothers of his *The Massacre of the Innocents*, which itself echoes passages of Marino's poem.[30] The story of Acis, completing the range of options between petrifaction and liquefaction, tells of a Sikelian youth who was changed into a river by his love Galatea to save him from the rock thrown by the jealous Polyphemus. Though not captured in such well-known images, the story was no less popular with contemporary poets.[31] The Neapolitan public will have been well-acquainted with Luis de Góngora's *La Fábula de Polifemo y Galatea*, published after the author's death in 1627. Coincidentally, Georg Friedrich Händel's cantata *Aci, Galatea e Polifemo*, first performed in Naples in 1708, was commissioned by Aurora Sanseverino.[32]

Barra concludes the discussion of his impressions of the grotto by referring to them as «feverish dreams, and tales of vain romances», a phrase borrowed from Francesco Berni's *Orlando innamorato* (published posthumously in the 1540s).[33] His description of these appearances as feverish dreams finds an interesting parallel in a passage of Daniello Bartoli's *Ricreazione del savio* of 1659. Bartoli describes man's dream world as a comedy with actors that are drunk and crazy, clothed in strange clothes and repulsive in their behaviour, while the scenes of this «comedy» change unexpectedly and at random and its story goes nowhere. The result is an exhibition so strange «that Ovid's and Apuleius' *Metamorphoses* and Lucian's *True History*, compared to our dreams, appear as the inventions of a wise man».[34] Bartoli goes on to compare the dream to the painter's grotesques, «a mosaic of irregularities put together».[35] Conversely, Daniele Barbaro, in his comments upon Vitruvius' treatise on architecture written almost a century earlier, likened the grotesque to the «confused images» of man's dreams.³⁶

Read in its original context, however, Berni's verse may be given a further significance. For it concludes a passage that invites the reader to «not stop at the outer bark, but look deeper within». The dream world conjured up by the author, with its dragons, beasts, giants, and «monsters with the faces of men» should be read as an allegory; a more profound message can be discovered between the lines.³⁷ Likewise, Barra points out that the marvel perceived by the senses immediately arouses the intellect which now takes central stage and attempts to unravel precisely how such phenomena occur.³⁸

The Art of Petrifaction

One of the few authors who has picked up on Barra's letter has been Giuseppe Antonini, baron of San Biaso, who mentions it briefly in his *La Lucania* of 1745. If only a footnote to his text, it is worth quoting here in full, also because apparently Antonini saw the grotto himself, and thus provides some indication that Barra was describing an actual cave.

> In Fossaceca, a place close to Venafro, several times I have had the pleasure of seeing a more than curious grotto under the mountain covered with cypress trees, in which [...] due to the water dripping from above, a very solid kind of alabaster is produced with thousands of jokes [*scherzi*], that soft at first, little by little grow harder, adding layer upon layer, as has been first observed with many learned considerations by the more than erudite *Signor* Simone Barra of Salerno, our friend...³⁹

The «thousands of jokes» mentioned by Antonini are jokes of nature, *ludi naturae*, the many figures described so eloquently by Barra.⁴⁰ No less interesting, however, is the context in which Antonini mentions the grotto, as it gives us the broader context in which Barra's interest in these phenomena can be understood. In his discussion of the river Sele (called Silaro by the author, from the Latin *Silarus*) Antonini notes how several ancient sources mention that any wood held in the river's water will turn to stone.⁴¹ This brings him to explore other examples of such rivers and lakes mentioned in ancient and modern sources, only to realize that nature today is not so generous with its wonders. Even so, Antonini does not refrain from referring to one, admittedly exotic, contemporary example: Abbé Rousseau's eyewitness account, discussed in his *Secrets et remedes éprouvez* of 1697, of melons, snakes, mushrooms, and wood, all petrified by having been buried for some time near the Red Sea.⁴²

As has been indicated by Antoine Schnapper, this interest in petrifaction could also be found in the early modern *Kunstkammer*, where petrified objects, ranging from sticks and plants to animals and whole human beings, often enjoyed pride of place.⁴³ At the same time, artists made casts of real animals and plants in bronze or other materials. We may point out, for example, the «flowers in silver, marvellously cast from life by Giovanni Palermo» that were to be seen in the treasury of the monastery of San Martino.⁴⁴ A scientific interest in processes of petrifaction can be found in the writings of the Sicilian painter Agostino Scilla, who, with his treatise on fossils published in Naples in 1670, provided an important step in the gradual acceptance of their animal origins.⁴⁵ For his careful analysis and groundbreaking depictions Scilla could rely on his own collection of petrified objects.⁴⁶ A related discussion is that of the origins of so-called *glossope-*

trae, or «tongue-stones»—in effect sharks' teeth. Already in 1616 the Neapolitan botanist and biologist Fabio Colonna would argue in his *De glossopetris dissertatio* that, rather than jokes of nature, these teeth were of animal origin.[47] Colonna's essay was published again in 1747 as an appendix to the Latin translation of Scilla's book.[48] About the process of petrifaction itself Scilla is brief, referring his reader to a small treatise about petrified crabs and snakes, written by the German scholar Johann Daniel Major.[49] Major, in his turn, draws attention to a petrified crab that was to be found in the Neapolitan collection of Ferrante Imperato, citing the eyewitness account of Johann Heinrich Pflaumern, who mentions it in his *Mercurius Italicus* among several other petrified *naturalia* in this «museum».[50] Also Fabio Colonna was well acquainted with Imperato's collection and the very same objects may have spurred his interest in the *glossopetrae*.[51]

The classic point of reference for such discussions of petrifaction is Ovid's tale of Perseus and Andromeda, or, more precisely, the tale of the origins of coral. When the hero lays down the snake-covered head of Medusa on a bed of seaweed in order to release Andromeda, the plants, «alive and porous to the core», harden at its touch. The sea-nymphs try this wonder on more plants, and scatter their seeds in the water. «Till this day», concludes Ovid, «the same nature has remained in coral so that it hardens when exposed to air».[52] A more dramatic account of the story was told by an anonymous ancient author going under the name of Orpheus in the hymn *Peri lithon* (On stones), first published in 1517 in both Greek and Latin.[53] Here, it is more explicitly Medusa's blood that is at the origins of coral:

> Still warm, still quivering, [he] lays his trophy down
> On the green sea-plants all about him strewn, [...]
> Pressed by the head the weeds around that lie
> Soaked with the gore, grow drunk with sanguine dye,
> The rushing breezes, daughters of the flood,
> Upon their boughs congeal the clotted blood,
> And so congeal, it seems, a real stone
> Nor only seems; to real rock 'tis grown.[54]

In his 1630 treatise on coral, the German physician Johann Ludwig Gans republished the passage on coral from *On stones*, adding no less than three Latin translations and notes to the text. In the main text of his book, Gans not only discusses the medical and magical application of coral, but also talks about its origins. For Gans, coral is a mineral from the very start that—and here, as we will see, we are close to Barra's theory about alabaster—becomes hard as a result of the salts it contains.[55] A review of the 1669 second edition of the book sums up his ideas as follows: «Coral is form'd out of a glutinous Juyce, which being turn'd into Stone by a salt, abounding in it, riseth up in the form of a Shrub.»[56] A similar thesis was put forward by Paolo Boccone, botanist to the Grand Duke of Florence and a good friend of Scilla, in his *Recherches et observations naturelles*, published in Amsterdam in 1674.[57] Opposing the idea of some that coral is in fact a petrified plant, Boccone argues that coral is produced by «*juxta position*, just as most types of stone», giving an important role to the *tartre coralin*, a wax-like substance, he finds at its extremities. For the present discussion, the letter by Mons. Pierre Guisony of Avignon, written in response to Boccone's thesis and published in his book, also is of interest. Referring to a specimen of coral in his *cabinet*, Guisony

1   Bernardo Cavallino, *The Triumph of Galatea*, c. 1650, oil on canvas, 148.3 × 203 cm, National Gallery of Art, Washington DC.

not only agrees with Boccone that coral belongs to the category of stones and is shaped by «a precipitation of various salts», but also adds that «[o]ne can see the same thing happen in some underground caves, where due to a continuous and long flow of drops of water, [...] branches of minerals are formed, and crystalline bodies in all kinds of shapes».[58]

Even if the story of the origins of coral is not depicted very often, it has spilled over into the domain of art too. Poussin's drawing *La tintura del corallo*, described by Giovan Pietro Bellori, is apparently an iconographic anomaly and appears to be based directly on the poetry of, again, Giovan Battista Marino.[59] A more indirect indication can be found in Bernardo Cavallino's extraordinary *Triumph of Galatea* in Washington, a work that stands out not only for the stunning nude of Galatea herself, but also for the meticulous rendering of the irregular crab shell and the fiery red coral.[60] (fig. 1) As has often been pointed out, these details are reminiscent of Neapolitan still-life painting.[61] Yet, in the present context, we may ask if particularly the coral should not be given a further significance.[62] For, in fact, the metamorphosis of coral from clothed blood to real stone described in *On Stones* is an exact reversal of that of Acis, where the blood running from his crushed body gradually turns to crystal clear water and flows back to the sea.[63] Thus, the coral may be said to refer to what is not seen in the picture, alluding to the metamorphosis of Acis and his invisible presence among the waves under which the coral is born. And finally, Galatea's pearl earring too would have reminded the beholder of such a process of transformation, a process meticulously described by Felice Stocchetti in his letter «on the generation of pearls», published, like that of Barra, in Bulifon's *Lettere memorabili*.[64]

71

Among these petrifactions and liquefactions, there is one phenomenon that stands out for its absence. For indeed, a very similar metamorphosis took place right before the eyes of the people of Naples: that of the liquefaction of the blood of the city's patron saint San Gennaro. It is hardly imaginable that this miracle did not enter Barra's mind—further indications of this will be touched upon below—but including it in his discussion would have been a dangerous step to take. As the author of an early eighteenth-century biography of the saint writes, some heretical authors had sought to find a scientific explanation, a «natural cause» for the miracle. What these authors had so «foolishly dreamt», however, was easily proven false.[65]

The «Enlivening Aura» of Sulphur

As the letter shows, Barra was interested in natural causes. Although this is not the place to fully explore the author's scientific arguments, some interesting aspects may be highlighted here. First of all, his main thesis suggests a central role for sulphur. As the author himself realizes, his idea is rather daring. This becomes all the more apparent when we read Felice Stocchetti's account of the generation of alabaster in his *Ragionamenti* of 1705. Spurred on by Barra's letter, Stocchetti visited the cave himself, but while he praises Barra's philosophical insights, he makes no mention of the author's central thesis; for Stocchetti, sulphur plays no role at all.[66]

And yet, Barra upholds his thesis, arguing that «an enlivening aura of the purest sulphur» emanates from the earth, changing when it comes into contact with air as it binds with its «seeds», the *semi dell'aria*.[67] Barra envisions sulphur as a substance with folding branches, thus capable of «embracing» the elements it encounters. Sulphur is accordingly at the origins of many minerals, adopting, «almost as a newborn Proteus», ever new forms as it binds with this or that particle.[68] Referring to the work of Torquato Tasso, Barra interprets the mythological battle between Typhon and Zeus as the confrontation between sulphur and air and finds here the origins of the «horrible spectacle» of the eruptions of the Etna and Vesuvius.[69] On a smaller scale, sulphur's capacity to enfold other elements is also at the origins of alabaster. Seeping through the pores [*forellini*] of the stone, sulphur binds the salts that are present in the water to form a soft substance, a *mollume*, that is similar to wet plaster and covers the stone throughout the cave. Here, indeed quite like the *tartre coralin* discussed by Boccone, the *mollume* slowly hardens into alabaster. Sulphur, Barra concludes, is not merely an ingredient of alabaster, «but its very architect».[70]

Barra's interest in sulphur can be explained rather easily, for at Pozzuoli, not too far from Naples, were the famous sulphur mines, the *solfatara*. That these were indeed avidly discussed at the table of Aurora Sanseverino may follow from the aforementioned letter on the «phenomena that are seen at the mountain of the sulphur mines near Pozzuoli». Written by Gregorio Caloprese and published by Bulifon in the same volume as Barra's letter, it is addressed to and written at the request of Nicolò Gaetani d'Aragona, Aurora's husband. The *solfatara* attracted the attention of artists too. Prints by or after the designs of Northern artists such as Joris Hoefnagel (1582), Stradanus (1587) and Joachim von Sandrart (1640) give an indication of the place's attraction for early modern tourists, while Anton Eisenhoit's engraving for Michele Marcator's *Metallotheca Vaticana*, an elaborate text about the collection of stones in the Vatican, points to the place's relevance for the context of natural science and the *Kunstkammer*.[71] Moreover, the *solfatara* brings us back to the issue of the divine as well, for it was here, according to tradition, that San Gennaro was beheaded. In this context, the *solfatara* showed up in local paintings as well. Among these, we may single out Aniello Falcone's rendering, which, according to the account of Sandrart, must have been in the famous Neapolitan collection of the Flemish merchant Gaspare Roomer.[72] De Dominici mentions in his *Vita* that Falcone depicted the location ‹al naturale›, thus suggesting that he made drawings on the spot.[73]

While this interest in the *solfatara* may have inspired Barra to give a central role to sulphur at all, he backs his thesis with evidence from a series of sources. His remark that not far from the grotto he has experienced «a very unpleasant smell, similar to that which one can experience at the sulphur mines» not only confirms his interest in the sulphur mines, but also indicates a central role for the senses in his approach. More striking is Barra's reference to sulphur's medical use.[74] Taking from the alabaster some of the *mollume*, a physician not mentioned by name found that the substance was endowed with a strong «corrective and diaphoretic virtue» and thus was very effective against fevers. This can only be explained, argues Barra, by the fact that it contains sulphur, for sulphur interacts with the blood and, due to its similarity to this *balsamo vitale*, cleans it of the corruptive «febrile matter».[75] A medical use of minerals was certainly not exceptional. Barra himself mentions the *oglio di sasso* found in Lombardy, now know as petroleum (from *petrae oleum*, «oil of stone»), and the medical use of coral, discussed at length in antique sources, was still central to Gans' treatise on coral mentioned above. Moreover, Pliny already recounts that ointments were thought to be conserved best in vessels of alabaster.[76] As Barra's argument makes clear, the processes of mineral metamorphosis quite easily extended into the study of the human body.

Barra's description and analysis of the alabaster cave proceeds on two levels: that of the imagination, and that of the intellect. What connects these two levels, is the central role of metamorphosis: on the level of the imagination we find the translucent stone and flowing water, slowly changing into ever so many figures; on that of the intellect we find the sulphur, that by enfolding other substances with its branches takes on ever new forms. By giving such a central role to sulphur, Barra appears to be searching for a natural foundation of a world always in flux, a world, moreover, that seems to have no place for a higher being. At the end of his letter he suggests that sulphur actually might fulfil this role: «maybe [sulphur] is that, which contains in itself the very idea of the seed of things, that is, their shaping virtue».[77] By relating to contemporaneous discussions of the *semina rerum*, the seeds of things, Barra takes his experiences in the grotto to a more universal level.[78] Yet, even this hesitant abstraction is grounded in an image: that of the branched substance that enfolds in order to take on new forms. It is an image that is coral-like, an image that belongs to the *Kunstkammer*. It was the *Kunstkammer* that provoked this interest in material and metamorphosis, but while such collections sometimes took on the shape of artificial grottoes, Barra's grotto was the real thing.[79] Here, in this Arcadian landscape, a hint of the formative power of the elements has been found, while the intellect is roused by images— Daphne, Niobe, Acis—that challenge the boundaries between art and nature.

Annotations

The author wishes to thank Robert Felfe, Elsje van Kessel, and Kimberley Skelton.

1 Simone Barra, letter to Filippo Bulifon, dated Piedimonte, 28 January 1696, in: *Lettere memorabili*, ed. by Antonio Bulifon, raccolta 4, Napoli 1698, p. 224–243.
2 Bulifon 1698 (as note 1), racc. 4, p. 225.
3 Bulifon 1698 (as note 1), racc. 3, p. 138–168, 176–185; id., racc. 4, p. 177–188.
4 Pamela H. Smith, «Art, Science, and Visual Culture in Early Modern Europe», in: *Isis*, 2006, vol. 97, p. 95. More generally: Horst Bredekamp, *Antikensehnsucht und Maschinenglauben: Die Geschichte der Kunstkammer und die Zukunft der Kunstgeschichte*, Berlin 1993.
5 Bernardo De Dominici, *Vite de' pittori, scultori ed architetti napoletani*, ed. by Fiorella Sricchia and Andrea Zezza, Napoli 2003–2008, vol. 3. 2, p. 1350.
6 Michele Maylender, *Storia delle accademie d'Italia*, Bologna 1929, vol. 5, p. 141. Barra chose the name Carisio.
7 Bulifon 1698 (as note 1), vol. 1, ed. 4, unnumbered page after the dedication; *Il Caprario: Accademie di alcuni rimatori, che nel medesimo monte si radunarono*, Napoli 1729 and Firenze 1732.
8 Gianfrancesco Trutta, *Dissertazioni istoriche delle antichità alifane*, Napoli 1776, p. 152–153. For Marzio Trutta see Francesco Maria Pratilli, *Della via Appia riconosciuta e descritta da Roma a Brindisi*, Napoli 1745, p. 419. Cf. Nicola Mancini, *Allifae*, Piedimonte Matese 1993, p. 39.
9 Valentina Lotoro, *La fortuna della «Gerusalemme liberata» nella pittura napoletana tra Seicento e Settecento*, Roma 2008, p. 79–102; Pietro Andrisani, «Aurora Sanseverino mecenate. Suo contributo allo sviluppo dell'opera in Scuola Napoletana», in: *Fardella 1704–2004: Tracce di storia*, ed. by Antonio Appella and Antonietta Latronico, Fardella 2004, p. 79–98; Ausilia Magaudda and Danilo Costantini, «Aurora Sanseverino (1669–1726) e la sua attività di committente musicale nel regno di Napoli. Con notizie inedite sulla napoletana congregazione dei sette dolori», in: *Giacomo Francesco Milano ed il ruolo dell'aristocrazia nel patrocinio delle attività musicali nel secolo XVIII*, ed. by Gaetano Pitarresi, Reggio Calabria 2001, p. 297–415.
10 De Dominici 2003–2008 (as note 5), vol. 3.1, p. 26, 454. Cf. Gérard Labrot, *Collections of Paintings in Naples 1600–1780*, München 1992, p. 422–423, 453, n. 21, 26, 152.
11 De Dominici 2003–2008 (as note 5), vol. 3.1, p. 314. For Vinaccia and Neapolitan sculpture in silver see Elio Catello and Corrado Catello, *Scultura in argento nel Sei e Settecento a Napoli*, Sorrento 2000, p. 27–57, with further references in n. 29.

12 Elio Catello, «Gian Domenico Vinaccia e il paliotto di San Gennaro», in: *Napoli nobilissima*, 1979, vol. 18, 1979, p. 121–132.
13 Johann Rudolf Glauber, *Tractatus de natura salium*, Amsterdam 1658, p. 5–6, 43. Cf. Pamela H. Smith, *The Body of the Artisan: Art and Experience in the Scientific Revolution*, Chicago 2004, p. 169; Ferdinando Abbri, «Gli ‹arcana naturae›: Filosofia, alchimia e ‹chimica› nel Seicento», in: *Cristina di Svezia: Scienza ed alchimia nella Roma barocca*, ed. by Wilma Di Palma et al., Bari 1990, p. 55–56.
14 A similar point has been made about Benvenuto Cellini's saltcellar now in Vienna; see Marina Belozerskaya, «Cellini's *Saliera*: The Salt of the Earth at the Table of the King», in: *Benventuo Cellini: Sculptor, Goldsmith, Writer*, ed. by Margaret Ann Gallucci and Paolo L. Rossi, Cambridge 2004, p. 71–96; Michael Cole, *Cellini and the Principles of Sculpture*, Cambridge 2002, p. 15–42.
15 See e.g., Vittorio Giovardi, *Notizia del nuovo teatro degli Arcadi aperto in Roma l'anno 1726*, Roma 1727, p. 33. Cf. Vernon Hyde Minor, *The Death of the Baroque and the Rhetoric of Good Taste*, Cambridge 2006, p. 146 ff. More generally, Helen Langdon, «A Theatre of Marvels. The Poetics of Salvator Rosa», in: *Konsthistorisk Tidskrift*, 2004, vol. 73, p. 179–192.
16 Jennifer Montagu, «Antonio and Gioseppe Giorgetti: Sculptors to Cardinal Francesco Barberini», in: *The Art Bulletin*, 1970, vol. 52, p. 280, n. 19. Cf. e. g., Olga Raggio, «The Farnese Table: A Rediscovered Work by Vignola», in: *The Metropolitan Museum of Art Bulletin*, 1960, vol. 18, p. 213–231.
17 Lavinio Quebà e Tuna, *Il fior fenice cioè Marzio redivivo in Gio: Francesco Cardinali Ginetti*, Venetia 1687, p. 381. For the chapel see Patrizia Cavazzini, «The Ginetti Chapel at S. Andrea della Valle», in: *The Burlington Magazine*, 1999, vol. 141, p. 401–413 (quoting Quebo e Tuna at n. 25) and Hellmut Hager, «Un riesame di tre cappelle di Carlo Fontana», *Commentari*, 1976, vol. 27, p. 252–289.
18 See for example, *Hans von Aachen (1552–1615). Hofkünstler in Europa*, ed. by Thomas Fusenig, Berlin and München 2010, p. 196–199. I thank Jannis Hadjinicolaou for discussing these works with me.
19 From the inventory of 1707 in: Archivio di Stato, Napoli, scheda 665, protocollo 52, f. 777 recto. The inventory is available through the online Getty Provenance Index Database. Elisabetta Vandeneynden inherited part of the collection of her father, the Flemish merchant Ferdinand Vandeneynden. See Renato Ruotolo, *Mercanti-collezionisti Fiamminghi a Napoli: Gaspare Roomer e i Vandeneynden*, Massa Lubrense 1982.

20 Bulifon 1698 (as note 1), racc. 4, p. 229.
21 Susanne König-Lein, «Ein Spiel der Natur? Bildersteine und Steinbilder», in: *Spiel, Kunst, Glück. Die Wette als Leitlinie der Entscheidung. Beispiele aus Vergangenheit und Gegenwart in Kunst, Wissenschaft, Wirtschaft*, ed. by Johann Konrad Eberlein, Wien 2011, p. 133–144.
22 Athanasius Kircher, *Mundus subterraneus*, Amsterdam 1665, vol. 2, p. 23–45. Ulisse Aldrovandi, *Musaeum metallicum*, Bologna 1648.
23 David Summers, «Michelangelo on Architecture», in: *The Art Bulletin*, 1972, 54, p. 146–157. For a more general discussion see: Philippe Morel, *Les grotesques: Les figures de l'imaginaire dans la peinture italienne de la fin de la Renaissance*, Paris 1997.
24 For examples of such descriptions, see some of the documents published in *Cosimo Fanzago e il marmo commesso fra Abruzzo e Campania nell'età barocca*, ed. by Vittorio Casale, L'Aquila 1995. Cf. John Nicholas Napoli, «Pianificare o indulgere nel capriccio? Cosimo Fanzago e la causa ‹ad exuberantiam› alla certosa di San Martino», in: *Napoli nobilissima*, 2003, Bd. 5, p. 209–218; Roberto Pane, «Marmi mischi e aggiunte a Cosimo Fanzago», in: *Seicento napoletano*, Milano 1984, p. 100–138; Annemarie Winther, *Cosimo Fanzago und die Neapler Ornamentik des 17. und 18. Jahrhunderts*, Bremen 1973.
25 Carlo De Lellis, *Aggiunta alla Napoli sacra del D'Engenio*, ed. by Francesco Aceto, Napoli 1977, p. 358. For an analysis of the artist's formal repertoire see Winther 1973 (as note 24), chapter 4.
26 Giovan Battista Francolo in Ireneo della Croce, *Historia antica e moderna, sacra e profana della città di Trieste*, Venetia 1698, p. 29.
27 Bulifon 1698 (as note 1), racc. 4, p. 230.
28 See Joris van Gastel, «Bernini's Metamorphosis: Sculpture, Poetry, and the Embodied Beholder», *Word & Image*, 2012, vol. 28, p. 193–205 (with further references).
29 Giovan Battista Marino, *Dicerie sacre e La strage de gl'innocenti*, ed. by Giovanni Pozzi, Torino 1960, p. 557–558.
30 Gabriele Wimböck, *Guido Reni (1575–1642). Funktion und Wirkung des religiösen Bildes*, Regensburg 2002, p. 182–184; Francis Haskell and Nicholas Penny, *Taste and the Antique: The Lure of Classical Sculpture*, New Haven and London 1981, no. 66; Elizabeth Cropper, «Marino's *Strage degli innocenti*: Poussin, Rubens, and Guido Reni», in: *Studi secenteschi*, 1992, Bd. 33, p. 137–164. For Marino's influence in Naples, among others on Massimo Stanzione's *The Massacre of the Innocents*, see: Sebastian Schütze, «Pittura parlante e poesia taciturna: Il ritorno di Giovan Battista Marino a Napoli, il suo concetto di imitazione e una mirabile interpretazione pittorica», in: *Documentary Culture: Florence and Rome from Grand-Duke Ferdinand I to Pope Alexander VII*, ed. by Elizabeth Cropper, Giovanna Perini and Francesco Solinas, Bologna 1992, p. 209–226.
31 Maria Teresa Graziosi, *Polifemo e Galatea: Mito e poesia*, Roma 1984, in particular, p. 85–151. Luca Giordano has painted several versions of the *Triumph of Galatea* where Acis' transformation can be seen; cf. Oreste Ferrari and Giuseppe Scavizzi, *Luca Giordano: l'opera completa*, Napoli 1992, cat.nos. A229, A230, A309. Another version is in the State Hermitage Museum, St. Petersburg.
32 Carlo Vitali and Antonello Furnari, «Händels Italienreise – neue Dokumente, Hypothesen und Interpretationen», in: *Göttinger Händel-Beiträge*, 1991, Bd. 4, p. 41–66.
33 Bulifon 1698 (as note 1), racc. 4, p. 230; Francesco Berni, *Orlando innamorato* [Venetia 1545], in: *Francesco Berni*, ed. by Raffaele Nigro, Roma 1999, p. 753 (I, xxv.6).
34 Daniello Bartoli, *La ricreazione del savio*, ed. by Bice Mortara Garavelli, Parma 1992, p. 343–344.
35 Ibid., p. 344.
36 Daniele Barbaro, *I Dieci libri dell'architettura di M. Vitruvio*, Venetia 1567, p. 321.
37 Berni 1999 (as note 33), p. 753 (I, xxv.6), 752 (I, xxv.2). Cf. Antonio Corsaro, «Fortuna e imitazione nel Cinquecento», in: *I Triumphi di Francesco Petrarca*, ed. by Claudia Berra, Bologna 1999, p. 456 ff.; Danilo Romei, «L'*Orlando* moralizzato dal Berni», in: *Banca dati «Nuovo Rinascimento»*, 1997, www.nuovorinascimento.org (accessed 1 May 2012), p. 13.
38 Bulifon 1698 (as note 1), racc. 4, p. 230–231.
39 Giuseppe Antonini, *La Lucania*, Napoli 1795, p. 183, n. 1. The town of Fossaceca is now named Fontegreca.
40 See *Ludi naturae: Spiele der Natur in Kunst und Wissenschaft*, ed. by Natascha Adamowsky, Hartmut Böhme, and Robert Felfe, Paderborn 2011; Paula Findlen, «Jokes of Nature and Jokes of Knowledge: The Playfulness of Scientific Discourse in Early Modern Europe», in: *Renaissance Quarterly*, 1990, vol. 43, p. 292–331.
41 For this discussion see Antonini 1795 (as note 39), p. 181–185.
42 Ibid., p. 183; cf. Abbé Henri de Montbazon Rousseau, *Secrets et remedes éprouvez*, Paris 1697, p. 186.
43 Antoine Schnapper, *Le géant, la licorne et la tulipe: Collections et collectionneurs dans la France du XVIIe siècle*, vol. 1, Paris 1988, p. 17–18. Cf. e.g., Paolo Maria Terzago and Pietro F. Scarabelli, *Museo ò galeria adunata dal sapere e dallo studio del Sig. canonico Manfredo Settala*, Tortona 1666, p. 75–82.
44 Domenico Antonio Parrino, *Napoli città nobilissima, antica e fedelissima, esposta agli*

75

occhi et alla mente de' curiosi, Napoli 1700, p. 124.
45 Agostino Scilla, *La vana speculazione disingannata dal senso,* ed. by Marco Segala, introduction by Paolo Rossi, Firenze 1996.
46 Sebastiano Di Bella, «Agostino Scilla collezionista: La raccolta di fossili», in: *Wunderkammer siciliana: Alle origini del museo perduto,* ed. by Vincenzo Abbate, Napoli 2001, p. 61–66. Also the collection of the painter Filippo Napoletano is interesting in this context; cf. Jennifer Fletcher, «Filippo Napoletano's Museum», in: *The Burlington Magazine,* 1979, vol. 121, p. 649–650.
47 Fabio Colonna, *De purpura,* Romae 1616, p. 31–39.
48 Agostino Scilla and Fabio Colonna, *De corporibus marinis lapidescentibus quæ defossa re periuntur; addita dissertatione F. Columnæ de glossopetris,* Romae 1747.
49 Ibid., p. 57; Johann Daniel Major, *Dissertatio epistolica de cancris et serpentibus petrefactis,* Jenae 1664. Later, Major would edit an edition of Colonna's *De purpura,* including also the *De glossopetris dissertatio;* see Fabio Colonna, *Opusculum de purpura,* ed. by Johann Daniel Major, Kiliae 1675.
50 Major 1675 (as note 49), p. 6; Johann Heinrich von Pflaumern, *Mercurius italicus,* Ulmue 1650, part 2, p. 65. For Imperato see: Enrica Stendardo, *Ferrante Imperato: Collezionismo e studio della natura a Napoli tra Cinque e Seicento,* Napoli 2001.
51 Cf. Colonna 1616 (as note 47), p. 36.
52 Ovid, *Metamorphoses,* translated by Frank Justus Miller, London 1916, vol. 1, p. 231.
53 *Mousaiou Poiemation ta kath' Hero kai Leandron. Orpheos Argonautika. Tou autou Hymnoi Orpheus peri lithon. Musæi opusculum de Herone & Leandro. Orphei argonautica. Eiusdem hymni. Orpheus de lapidibus,* Venezia 1517.
54 Translation from Charles William King, *The Natural History, Ancient and Modern, of Precious Stones and Gems, and of the Precious Metals,* London 1865, p. 390.
55 Johann L. Gans, *Corallorum historia,* Francofurti 1630; cf. Schnapper 1988 (as note 43), p. 22.
56 *Philosophical Transactions,* 1670, vol. 5, p. 1200 (=1202).
57 Paolo Boccone, *Recherches et observations naturelles,* Amsterdam 1674, p. 24–42. Boccone recommends Gans' book on p. 43. For his friendship with Scilla see Scilla 1996 (as note 45), p. 35 & 53. For Boccone see Isabella Sermonti Spada, «Boccone, Paolo (in religione frate Silvio)», in: *Dizionario Biografico degli Italiani,* vol. 11, Roma 1969; Bruno Accordi, «Paolo Boccone (1633–1740): A Practically Unknown Excellent Geo-Paleontologist of the 17th Century», in: *Geologica Romana,*1975, vol. 14, p. 353–359.
58 Boccone 1674 (as note 57), p. 22.

59 Richard E. Spear, «The Literary Source of Poussin's Realm of Flora», in: *The Burlington Magazine,* 1965, vol. 107, p. 566; cf. Giovan Pietro Bellori, *Le vite de' pittori, scultori e architetti moderni,* ed. by Evelina Borea, Torino 1976, p. 458. Poussin's drawing, in turn, inspired Claude Lorrain's painting of the same subject, made for Cardinal Camillo Massimi who also owned Poussin's drawing. Linda Lee Boyer, «The Origin of Coral by Claude Lorrain», in: *The Metropolitan Museum of Art Bulletin,* 1968, vol. 26, p. 370–379.
60 *Bernardo Cavallino of Naples, 1616–1656,* ed. by Ann Lurie, Bloomington 1984, cat. no. 68. An attribution to Artemisia Gentileschi, first proposed by Józef Grabski, «On Seicento Painting in Naples: Some Observations on Bernardo Cavallino, Artemisia Gentileschi and Others», in: *Artibus et Historiae,* 1985, vol. 6, p. 41–55, has more recently been convincingly rebutted by Christopher R. Marshall, «An Early Inventory Reference and New Technical Information for Bernardo Cavallino's ‹Triumph of Galatea›», in: *The Burlington Magazine,* 2005, vol. 147, p. 40–44. Marshall's suggestion that the Washington painting may be the one mentioned in the inventory of Carlo Arcici, however, seems unlikely; cf. Giuseppe De Vito, «A Note on Artemisia Gentileschi and Her Collaborator Onofrio Palumbo», in: *The Burlington Magazine,* 2005, vol. 147, p. 749.
61 For Neapolitan still life painting see *L'œil gourmand: Parcours dans la nature morte napolitaine du XVIIe siècle,* ed. by Véronique Damian, Paris 2007.
62 On the use of coral in Naples see Gina Carla Ascione, *Storia del corallo a Napoli dal XVI al XIX secolo,* Napoli 1991.
63 Ovid 1916 (as note 52), vol. 2, p. 290 (XIII. 885–897). In Góngora the transformation is more abrupt; cf. Luis Góngora y Argote, *The Fable of Polyphemus and Galatea,* translated and analyzed by Miroslov John Hanak, New York 1988, p. 197–201.
64 Bulifon 1698 (as note 1), racc. 3, p. 138–168; Stocchetti also refers to coral here, cf. p. 149.
65 Girolamo Maria, *Istoria della vita, virtù, e miracoli di S. Gennaro vescovo, e martire,* Napoli 1707, p. 135–136.
66 Felice Stocchetti, *Ragionamenti intorno alla pressione dell'aria, a' surgimenti de' liquori e ad altri sollevamenti de' fluidi entro cannonelli di svariata figura,* Venezia 1705, p. 20–21.
67 Bulifon 1698 (as note 1), racc. 4, p. 232.
68 Bulifon 1698 (as note 1), racc. 4, p. 233.
69 Valeria Merola, «La fortuna del mito dell'Etna tra Cinquecento e Seicento», in: *Spazi, geografie, testi,* ed. by Siriana Sgavicchia, Roma 2004, p. 59–71.
70 Bulifon 1698 (as note 1), racc. 4, p. 237.

71 See Lucia Nuti, «The Mapped Views by Georg Hoefnagel: The Merchant's Eye, the Humanist's Eye», in: *Word & Image*, 1988, vol. 4, p. 568; Alessandra Baroni Vannucci, *Jan van der Straet, detto Giovanni Stradano, flandrus pictor et inventor*, Milano 1997, no. 786; Anna Schreurs, *Joachim von Sandrart (1606–1688). Ein europäischer Künstler aus Frankfurt*, Frankfurt a.M. 2006, p. 19–21; *Wunderwerk. Göttliche Ordnung und vermessene Welt. Der Goldschmied und Kupferstecher Antonius Eisenhoit und die Hofkunst um 1600*, ed. by Christoph Stiegemann, Mainz 2003, p. 145, 153.

72 Achille Della Ragione, *Aniello Falcone: Opera completa*, Napoli 2008, p. 44. For Roomer's collection see Ruotolo 1982 (as note 19), and for his interest in Falcone, Annachiara Alabiso, «Aniello Falcone's Frescoes in the Villa of Gaspar Roomer at Barra», in: *The Burlington Magazine*, 1989, vol. 131, p. 31–36.

73 Dominici 2003–2008 (as note 5), vol. 3.1, p. 132. A drawing of the Solfatara by Falcone is in a private collection in Switzerland; cf. *Civiltà del Seicento a Napoli*, ed. by Silvia Cassani, Napoli 1984, p. 86, no. 3.30.

74 Bulifon 1698 (as note 1), racc. 4, p. 235.

75 Bulifon 1698 (as note 1), racc. 4, p. 237. Some ancient sources for the medical use of alabaster are mentioned in Giacinto Gimma, *Della storia naturale delle gemme, delle pietre e di tutti minerali, ovvero della fisica sotterranea*, Napoli 1730, vol. 2, p. 12.

76 Pliny the Elder, *Natural History*, translated by D.E. Eichholz, Cambridge (MA) 1962, vol. 10, 36.12; cf. Gimma 1730 (as note 75), vol. 2, p. 10.

77 Bulifon 1698 (as note 1), racc. 4, p. 242.

78 Hiro Hirai, *Le concept de semence dans les théories de la matière à la Renaissance de Ficin à Gassendi*, Turnhout 2005; Antonio Clericuzio, *Elements, Principles and Corpuscles. A study of Atomism and Chemistry in the Seventeenth Century*, Dordrecht 2000. In relation to art: Robert Felfe, «Geordnetes Weltgebäude oder ‹lusus atomorum›? Visuelle Dynamiken physikotheologischer Naturzuwendung», in: *Die Welt im Bild. Weltentwürfe in Kunst, Literatur und Wissenschaft seit der Frühen Neuzeit*, ed. by Ulrike Gehring, München 2010, p. 145–176.

79 Stephanie Hanke, «The Splendour of Bankers and Merchants: Genoese Garden Grottoes of the Sixteenth Century», in: *Urban History*, 2010, vol. 37, p. 399–418. More general, Philippe Morel, *Les grottes maniéristes en Italie au XVIe siècle: Théâtre et alchimie de la nature*, Paris 1998.

AutorInnen dieses Heftes

Robert Felfe ist wissenschaftlicher Mitarbeiter an der Kolleg-Forschergruppe *Bildakt und Verkörperung* an der Humboldt-Universität zu Berlin. Schwerpunkte seiner Forschungen sind Sammlungen der Frühen Neuzeit, Kunst und Naturwissen sowie Praxis und Theorie der Druckgrafik. Zu seinen Publikationen in diesem Bereich gehören: *Ludi Naturae. Spiele der Natur in Kunst und Wissenschaft*, hg. mit Natascha Adamowsky u. Hartmut Böhme (München 2011); «‹Naer het leven›. Eine sprachliche Formel zwischen bildgenerierenden Übertragungsvorgängen und ästhetischer Vermittlung», in: *Ad Fontes! Niederländische Kunst des 17. Jahrhunderts in Quellen*, hg. v. Claudia Fritzsche u.a. (Petersberg 2012).

Joris van Gastel is research fellow at the Kolleg-Forschergruppe Bildakt und Verkörperung at the Humboldt Univeristät, Berlin. He studied art history and psychology at the VU University Amsterdam and the Università Ca' Foscari in Venice. His research focuses on Italian Renaissance and Baroque sculpture, the psychology of art and Baroque Naples. Publications include: «Bernini's Metamorphosis: Sculpture, Poetry, and the Embodied Beholder», in: *Word & Image* 28/2 (2012), and «Hoc Opus Exculpsit Io. Bologna. Andreas Andreanus Incisit: Andrea Andreani's chiaroscuro houtsneden naar Giambologna», in: *The Rijksmuseum Bulletin*, 55/1 (2007).

Henrike Haug ist wissenschaftliche Mitarbeiterin am Institut für Kunstwissenschaft und Historische Urbanistik der TU Berlin. Ihr gegenwärtiger Arbeitsschwerpunkt sind Relationen zwischen der Werkstattpraxis von Goldschmieden und Naturforschung im 16./17. Jahrhundert. Zu ihren Publikationen gehören: «Materie als Prinzip und Ursache der Individuation. Ähnlichkeit und Bildnis in der Plastik des 13. Jahrhunderts», in: *Similitudo. Konzepte der Ähnlichkeit in Mittelalter und Früher Neuzeit*, hg. v. Martin Gaier u.a. (München 2012); «Rechtssicherheit durch Kunst-Beschreibung. Die Beispiele von Saint-Denis, Stablo und San Clemente in Casauria», in: *Visibilität des Unsichtbaren. Sehen und Verstehen in Mittelalter und Früher Neuzeit*, hg. v. Anja Lutz (Zürich 2011).

Nikola Irmer studierte bildende Kunst am San Francisco Art Institute, an der Glasgow School of Art und am Hunter College New York. Seit 2000 lebt sie als Malerin und Zeichnerin in Berlin. Ein Schwerpunkt ihrer Arbeit ist das Porträt; seit 2008 beschäftigt sie sich zudem mit naturkundlichen Sammlungen und deren Geschichte. Die Arbeiten von Nikola Irmer wurden unter anderem in New York, Berlin, London, Köln und Hamburg ausgestellt. Ihr Projekt *Promethean Boldness* wurde zur *dOCUMENTA (13)* eingeladen und ist hier Teil des „Worldly House", eines Künstler-Archivs, inspiriert von Donna Haraway und kuratiert von Tue Greenfort.

Claudia Swan is Associate Professor of early modern Northern European Art History at Northwestern University (Evanston, IL, USA). Her research interests include Netherlandish art, the visual culture of natural history, the history of collection, Renaissance and Baroque graphic arts, and the history of the imagination. She is completing a book on *Exoticism at Work in Early Modern Holland*, a portion of which is forthcoming in Fall 2012 in *De Zeventiende Eeuw*, titled «Birds of Paradise for the Sultan: Early Seventeenth-Century Dutch-Turkish Encounters and the Uses of Wonder».

Bildnachweise

Editorial
S. 2 Ulisse Aldrovandi, *Musaeum Metallicum*, Bologna 1648, S. 765, Detail.
S. 4 Streekarchivariaat Noordwest-Veluwe, archief stadsbestuur Harderwijk, OAH 2037 46r.
S. 20 Naturabgüsse einer Schlange und einer Kröte, Blei/Zinn bzw. Bronze, 16. Jh., Kunsthistorisches Museum Wien, Kunstkammer, in: *Täuschend echt...*, hg. v. Ortrud Westheider und Michael Philipp, Hamburg/München 2010, S. 78.
S. 48 Imago B. Mariae Virginis cum Filiolo in minera ferri expressa, in: Miscellanea, 1670, Bd. 1, S. 265.
S. 64 Salvator Rosa, *A Man Seen from Behind*, c. 1656–1657, etching, British Museum, London © Trustees of the British Museum.

Swan
1–2 Streekarchivariaat Noordwest-Veluwe, archief stadsbestuur Harderwijk.

Felfe
1 Joseph Furttenbach, *Architectura privata...*, Augsburg 1641, Tab. 11, Detail.

Irmer
Copyright Nikola Irmer.

Haug
1 Henrike Haug
2–3 Sächsische Landesbibliothek – Staats- und Universitätsbibliothek Dresden, Digitale Sammlungen.
4 *Der silberne Boden. Kunst und Bergbau in Sachsen*, hg. v. Manfred Bachmann, Harald Marx und Eberhard Wächtler, Leipzig 1990, Kat Nr. 322, S. 182.

Van Gastel
1 Image: National Gallery of Art, Washington.

Neuerscheinung

Jonas Verlag

Peer Zickgraf
Völkerschau und Totentanz
Deutsches (Körper-)Weltentheater
zwischen 1905 und heute

ISBN 978-3-89445-468-5
144 Seiten, 72 Abbildungen
Broschur, 20 Euro
Format 17 × 24 cm

Dieses Buch ist eine Reise in Zwischenreiche. Es erkundet zoologische Gärten, in denen Menschen aus Kolonialgebieten bis in die 30er Jahre des 20. Jahrhunderts zusammen mit exotischen Tieren ausgestellt wurden. Doch die Faszination und die Zurschaustellung des „Fremden", „Anderen", die in den Völkerschauen exotisch verklärend inszeniert wird, ist nur die eine Seite. In den deutschen Kolonien erfährt das „Fremde" in seiner konkreten körperlichen Realität durch Tötung, Ausbeutung, Kolonisierung und kulturelle Assimilation eine Behandlung, die auf sein Verschwinden abzielt. Insbesondere wurden Mediziner in dem kolonialen rechtsfreien Raum aktiv, indem sie großangelegte medizinische Versuche an der Bevölkerung durchführten. Viele dieser ehemaligen aufstrebenden Tropenärzte fanden später im Nationalsozialismus ein Umfeld, in dem sie ihre Menschenversuche, nun in den deutschen Konzentrationslagern, fortführen konnten.
Nach 1989, in einem negativ aufgeladenen kulturellen und politischen Klima, betrat Gunter von Hagens mit seinen „Körperwelten" plötzlich die Bühne. Mit seinen toten Körpern, die er gleich Frankenstein erschafft und jeglicher Würde beraubt, feiert er beim staunenden Publikum große Erfolge. Peer Zickgraf geht in seinem Buch den Mechanismen nach, die diesen Umgang mit dem Körper auslösen.

Jonas Verlag für Kunst und Literatur GmbH · Weidenhäuser Strasse 88 · D-35037 Marburg
Telefon 06421-25132 · Fax 06421-210572 · jonas@jonas-verlag.de · www.jonas-verlag.de